WARRIOR MATERIAL

By

MARIOS ELLINAS

For Worldwide Distribution, Printed in the U.S.A.

ISBN: 978-0-615-33826-2

Warrior Material

By Marios Ellinas

Published by Marios Ellinas

www.warriormaterial.com

maellinas@yahoo.com

Cover Design by **Tulip Graphics**
tulipgr@mweb.co.za

DEDICATION

I dedicate this book to the memory of Marie K. Cowell, who fought the good fight, finished the race, and kept the faith. I miss her!

ACKNOWLEDGEMENTS

I honor my wife, Danielle, for always modeling a passionate and uncompromising pursuit of intimacy with God. I am eternally grateful for her love, sweet spirit, and unfailing support. I love you, Danielle!

From the deepest part of me, I thank my children, Christos, Caleb, and Chloe, for being such wonderful kids. Along with their mother, they are my best friends. Their encounters with God, spirit of adventure, and excitement for life continually expand the boundaries of my imagination.

I give honor to my parents, Andreas and Irene Ellinas, as well as to Danielle's parents, Armand and Diane Chenelle, for being the best parents and grandparents. I thank them for their continual love and support — they are amazing!

I thank my aunt, Georgia Ellina-Papafoti, for her kindness and influence throughout my life. She is precious to me!

My brothers, Pericles and Antonis Ellinas, have been among the most encouraging voices in my life. I love them and thank them for their friendship. They are remarkable men!

I honor Dr. Gary Kellner for his outstanding leadership and impeccable example of humility and servant hood. I thank him for always believing in me and for making such a significant contribution through the *Foreword*.

An enormous '*Thank You*' to all my mentors and friends who submitted an endorsement for this book. Each of them has added great value to *Warrior Material* through his/her declaration over the work.

A loud shout-out to my *Valley Shore Assembly of God* church family. I love everyone so deeply. I commend all our staff, volunteers, and members for their relentless pursuit of God and for their commitment to revival.

My most heartfelt thanks to the following men who continually speak into my life in a mentoring capacity: *Pastor Ron Bradley, Pastor Nick Fatato, Pastor Glenn Harvison, Pastor Jan Nel, and Dr. Gary Kellner.* I hold them in the highest regard!

I honor my friend, Pastor James Baker, for forty-five years of faithful ministry in the town of Old Saybrook. His integrity, humility, and fatherly love are exemplary. He is a pillar in our town!

I thank Jason Westerfield for his friendship and support. His ministry and lifestyle cause me to fall deeper in love with Jesus, and to believe all things are possible through our God!

A huge thank-you goes out to Lauryn Feiler for helping me back on my feet, and for teaching me how to run "without wincing."

I salute Stephen and Laureen Moran and all my friends at Crossroads PT and Camp Care. I commend their exceptional commitment to people's healing and restoration. I am one such recipient of their love.

I thank my Green Beret comrades, Pambos Chrysostomou and Giorgos Chrysiliou, for twenty-one years of precious friendship. From the mountains of Cyprus to the streets of Larnaca, New York City, San Francisco, and beyond…they have remained "brothers in arms" throughout all seasons and changes.

I am grateful to Jason Hackley for editing the *Warrior Material* manuscript. He has demonstrated remarkable patience and diligence throughout the editing process.

Many thanks to Patrick Lynch for his assistance with transcription. I appreciate him for always having a heart to serve, and for serving this project joyfully.

I thank Peter Sylvester for formatting the manuscript, for helping with the distribution of the book online, and for his sound counsel on technical matters. He is a true servant!

ENDORSEMENTS

Get ready to throw off every weight that has held you back from seeing your God-dreams realized, and prepare to burst into your full potential as a son or daughter of The King!

A warrior himself, Marios will call your spirit to life with every page and hand you the keys to lay claim to your destiny in Christ. This is your time and it starts here!

Dan Macaulay
Worship Leader and Recording Artist

~ ~ ~

I have had the honor of walking very closely and intimately with Marios throughout the last several years leading up to the release of *Warrior Material*. Again and again, I have been impressed at his uncompromising commitment to pursue all of what God has for him, his family, and the church family he is stewarding. Marios is running with all of his strength for the advancement of his King and his King's Kingdom.

What you read in the pages to follow has developed in Marios through years of practical experience. The content has first been tested in Marios' life, then refined, improved upon, and now it is finally released for our benefit.

It is with my whole heart that I endorse Marios and *Warrior Material*. Words cannot express my value for this man of God, and I continue to thank the Lord for Marios' influence in my life, as well as our region and beyond!

Michael Manthei

~ ~ ~

Marios has written a book of impartation. It is not merely a dry discourse on a given subject; it is an impartation of life to bring us closer to Jesus, our Warrior King. We teach not what we know but who we are, and this is true of this soldier's handbook. It is written by a general who has not spent his time in the lofty corridors of government buildings, but in the thick of the battle, and has emerged victorious and full of courage all these years on.

Thanks, Marios, for engaging us in this journey and for equipping us more effectively for our own kingdom battles!

Fini de Gersigny
Founding Pastor
Jubilee International Church, Sydney, Australia

~ ~ ~

I have found that discouragement is the removal of courage from a person. It is a skill many have developed and exercise way too often. I have found that encouragement is dropping courage into a person's life. This, too, is a wonderful skill that we all treasure when we are the recipient of it.

Marios Ellinas is highly skilled in encouragement. My conversations with him, my observations of him, and the words he writes always encourage my life. This book is loaded with encouragement for all who will read. Read it and then you will go after God's assignment on your life!

Nick Fatato
Executive Director of Minister Development - SNED
Lead Pastor - Common Church, Boston, Massachusetts

~ ~ ~

Warrior Material is not a book; it is a Strategic Defense Manual. Marios has captured the heart-cry of the "Captain of our Salvation" and has led the way for many warriors to perfect the art of spiritual warfare. The Kingdom will certainly be "taken by force" as readers live out its practical message on the battlefield. This book is a must for every soldier's library!

Robert Keator
Lead Pastor
New Life Assembly, Griswold, Connecticut

~ ~ ~

Marios Ellinas' daily life reflects all the principles taught in this book. He uses timeless Biblical principles that can be used in everyone's life to succeed. If the Body of Christ would use the methods taught in this book, the Church would change. Each day, Christians face choices that, if made correctly, would result in transformation. This book is a reminder of what we can do when we face the battles of these choices. *Warrior Material* is a much needed book that gives the tools to be Spiritual Warriors on a daily basis. Every Christian can benefit from reading this book.

Barbara Lachance
President - Connecticut House of Prayer, Inc.
CEO - Generational Solutions, LLC

~ ~ ~

There are times in life when one encounters an unusual human who carries qualities that are unique! My meeting with Marios was one of those encounters. From the beginning, I was aware that he carried a presence and manner that set him apart from most men I meet in my travels.

My passion is identifying and developing men and women for ministry; and while training leaders in many nations, one becomes aware of unique individuals when they cross your path. What stands out to me is that Marios has identified some of the characteristics that set men and women apart as "Warriors", and to add to it, he embodies these elements in an increasing way in his own life.

As a fellow soldier in the natural and in the Lord, I find that this book merges the qualities of effective warriors in the natural and in the spiritual and gives us clear guidelines as to how to aim at these being built into our lives.

Jan Nel
www.teemnet.com

~ ~ ~

Jesus taught and spoke to His disciples in parables. In *Warrior Material,* Marios teaches and writes a parable that delves deep into the training and character strengths necessary for the Lord's warriors, the lions of Judah, rising up into that aspect of God, Jehovah-Sabaoth, the "Lord of Hosts". Marios, a former Special Forces warrior in the natural and a warrior in the Spirit, calls forth within the reader the Kingdom-advancing warrior spirit to overcome and bring victory in every realm and area of authority.

Marios, a pastor and laser arrow-piercing teacher/preacher, walks in and understands the apostolic governmental authority of the Lord that allows the Spirit to move in supernatural power and might. The clarity and multi-faceted strategic awareness exemplified in the Special Forces shines bright and illuminates the heart in this book through excellent writing, experiences, scriptural analogies, and the lasting fruit of the Spirit.

God is raising up His end-time army NOW! *Warrior Material* trains and equips the warriors of the Lord's army. Who do you want to be with in the midst of battle? First and foremost, the "The Lord of Hosts", the commander of the angelic host and the armies of God. Next, with a warrior and leader like Marios Ellinas. Only a true warrior with the compassionate heart of Jesus could write such a work. The understanding and impartation is deep and subtle!!

Yea God!

Janet LeBoutillier
Kingdom Watchmen, Kingdom Freedom
Cornelia Ministries, Inc.

~ ~ ~

FOREWORD

Marios Ellinas is a warrior.

Warriors are marked by focus, intensity and determination to achieve their objectives. They leave behind family and friends in the service of a cause. They are prepared to give what Abraham Lincoln called, "The last full measure of devotion."

Marios Ellinas has demonstrated warrior spirit all of his life.

When a Special Forces Major told him he was too small to become a Green Beret in the army of his native Cyprus, Marios risked court martial to pursue his dream. He possesses a passion and commitment one seldom sees in local church pastors. He understands, as few ministers do, that the Christian life is warfare and unless the believer cultivates the attitudes and disciplines of the warrior, he or she will certainly be defeated. Like all warriors, defeat is not an option for Marios.

Warrior Material is not just another Christian book in a market glutted with titles on self-realization, mood control and dieting; it is a call to arms, a practical manual that will help the reader become the person they want to be. Each chapter presents an indispensable element of the warrior's identity.

Don't just read this book. Think on it. Use it as a tool to evaluate where you are today, and a guide to help you set strategy to become the warrior you have been called to be.

Dr. Gary Kellner
President – International Center for Christian Leadership

Table of Contents

We are at war, always!

INTRODUCTION

The Bible places our brief, but very significant, earthly existence within the context of a great war between two kingdoms, the Kingdom of God and the kingdom of darkness. The war began when satan and one third of the angels were cast out of heaven after their failed attempt to usurp God's throne.

I have very little to say in this book about satan and his kingdom. I only recognize him as an evil, lying, and devious arch-enemy of whose devices we must be aware, yet an enemy who has been defeated once and for all.

When Jesus rose from the dead, He dealt the finishing blow to satan and all his minions. Through His blameless life, sacrifice on the cross, and especially through His resurrection, Christ redeemed mankind from sin, conquered death, and made eternal life available for all who believe in Him. Our enemy has lost. The only factor involved before the kingdom of darkness goes up in flames (literally) is time.

> God is never retreating. He is advancing; and the knowledge of His love, power, and glory is ever-increasing — one day it will cover the whole earth!

You and I are living somewhere during that span of time. Though the outcome of the war is certain, the confrontation between the two kingdoms continues daily. The battle lines are drawn and warriors are fighting, both naturally and supernaturally, within the confines of this earth as well as in the heavenly realms.

In addition to ultimately being victorious, God's Kingdom is continually advancing. God is not taking cover in a trench; He is not merely preserving and maintaining His ground; and most certainly, God is never retreating. He is advancing; and the knowledge of His love, power, and glory, is ever-increasing — one day it will cover the whole earth!

God advances His Kingdom, in large part, through individuals — people who love God and whose lives are committed to His ways, will, and purposes. And since such Kingdom-advancers are operating within the context of cosmic warfare, they are, in essence, warriors — *Kingdom* warriors.

What do Kingdom warriors look like?

Since the publication of my first book, *Running to the Impossible*, I have received much feedback regarding the illustrations I drew from my years of service in the Cypriot Special Forces. The remarks have been positive and somewhat amusing, especially those expressed by some of the elderly ladies from our congregation.

"We sure wouldn't have figured you to be one of those Marine, Ranger types, Pastor."

In other words, "You don't look like warrior material."

It's true—I don't.

If being considered a warrior for Christ is contingent upon satisfying the movie-generated stereotypes of bulging muscles, intense training, wilderness survival skills, close-combat tactics, knowledge of weapons, and head-to-toe camouflage while encroaching on enemy territory, then by all means count me out.

After almost two decades since my last day in uniform, I have forgotten most of the skills I acquired during my training. Rappelling is daunting; an obstacle course is definitely out; explosions are only for the movies; and though I can still hit the clay targets in the back yard with my sons' Daisy BB guns, I make about two out of five shots—a far shot (no pun intended) from my Green Beret sniper days!

As for physical fitness, I may not be in the worst shape imaginable, yet my fitness levels are nowhere near those of an elite warrior.

I am able to run for a few miles in the morning, but I surely pay for it through aches and pains the rest of the day. I can still perform a few hand-to-hand combat moves, yet when my two boys gang up on me, I quickly succumb.

> Being a Kingdom warrior is primarily about establishing and nurturing a relationship with the *King* of the Kingdom, Jesus.

From time to time, I compete with some of the teenagers or young adults from our church in doing push-ups. I always elicit some smirks from my opponents when I inform them I have to warm up first by stretching for five minutes. Worse yet, I have yet to win one such push-up contest.

Being a soldier in the army of our Lord has little to do with the physique or skill sets one may acquire over a few months of boot camp and then possibly forget over the course of the rest of his or her life. Being a Kingdom warrior is primarily about establishing and nurturing a relationship with the *King* of God's Kingdom, Jesus.

Long before Jesus was born, Daniel prophesied that Christ was preeminent over the Kingdom of God:

Then to Him was given dominion and glory and a kingdom that all peoples, nations, and languages should serve Him. His dominion is an everlasting dominion, which shall not pass away, and His kingdom the one which shall not be destroyed.
Daniel 7:14

Jesus' headship is also clearly stated in Paul's epistle to the Colossians:

He [God] has delivered us from the power of darkness and conveyed us into the kingdom of the Son of His love... All things were created through Him and for Him. And He is before all things, and in Him all things consist.
Colossians 1:13, 16-17

The verses following give insight as to why the Kingdom was granted to Jesus:

For it pleased the Father that in Him all the fullness should dwell, and by Him to reconcile all things to Himself, by Him, whether things on earth or things in heaven, having made peace through the blood of His cross.
Colossians 1:19-20

A prophetic picture in Revelation also shows Jesus as commander over God's army.

Now I saw heaven opened, and behold, a white horse. And He who sat on him was called Faithful and True, and in righteousness He judges and makes war. And the armies in heaven, clothed in fine linen, white and clean, followed Him on white horses.
Revelation 19:11, 14

Jesus rules and reigns over God's Kingdom, and He has command over the armies of heaven. He desires to have a very close relationship with every subject of the Kingdom, every warrior in His army.

Establishing a good relationship with a teacher will enhance our opportunities for learning. A good relationship with an entrepreneur will open doors for us in the business sector. The relationship between athletes and their coaches will be significant to their pursuit of a sports career.

Likewise, through our relationship with Jesus, our King and Supreme Commander, we obtain all the necessary attributes, principles, and properties for successfully waging war against the kingdom of darkness.

Each chapter of this book presents a key character quality Christ-followers nurture and cultivate as we continually pursue a personal, intimate relationship with God. The conglomerate of values, ideals, principles, and disciplines we obtain and uphold throughout our walk with Him constitute what I call, *Warrior Material.*

You and I have been born into a confrontation between Light and darkness. We are living on a vast and multi-dimensional battlefield, and the war is raging. God has made available to us "material" by which we can fight victoriously for His glory.

> God has made available to us "material" by which we can fight victoriously for His glory.

The qualities I present in the pages ahead are not the only ones considered Warrior Material. There are undoubtedly other building blocks to the Kingdom warrior's makeup. I am only presenting the attributes I have examined and experienced more closely.

I used to think I became a warrior at the close of a two-hour ceremony that followed my successful passage through Special Forces Selection. Since then, I have come to understand that the heart of a warrior was beating within me long before I ever enlisted. Special Forces training only served as a catalyst to activate the warrior within.

God has placed within you and me a warrior spirit, the part of us that loves God passionately and wholeheartedly; the force that drives us to relentlessly pursue God's will, God's purposes, and the advancement of His Kingdom.

Genesis 1:26 declares that all humanity is made in the image and likeness of God. Colossians 1:27 states that Christ, "the Hope of glory," lives inside every believer. Our warrior spirit reflects the image and likeness of our Heavenly Father as the Lord of Hosts, and the image and likeness of Jesus as the Ultimate Warrior and Commander of the armies of God.

> *Who is this King of glory? The Lord strong and mighty, the Lord mighty in battle...Who is this King of glory? The Lord of hosts, He is the King of glory.*
> Psalm 24:8, 10

When we battle against the forces of our adversary, our warrior spirit connects us with Christ's Warrior nature; and since He lives inside us, we co-labor.

Various influences in our lives, as well as adverse or hurtful circumstances, may have quenched or suppressed our warrior spirit. Poverty, infirmity, injuries, loss of loved ones, broken homes, control from domineering family members or leaders, lack of opportunities for education, and other limitations always war against the warrior within to hinder us from knowing God intimately and from maximizing our potential in Him.

I offer this book as a counter-offensive against all limitation; a means by which God will awaken, revive, activate, or strengthen our warrior spirit.

One day, my friend, Michael, and I were ministering to a man from our church. At the very end of our counseling session and prayer, Michael asked the man for permission to do something rather unusual.

"Sure," the man said. "What do you want to do?"

"I want to shout to your spirit man," Michael replied with a smile.

Once he obtained permission, Michael bent over until his head was right around the gentleman's abdomen. Then at the top of his lungs, he let out a cry — "Heeey!!!!!"

Michael smiled. The man smiled. I smiled as well. I knew exactly what Michael had accomplished. He had called the warrior inside our brother out of limitation and dormancy into battle.

Within just a few days from the incident, the man we ministered to was bearing fruit of transformation. His demeanor, decisions, and actions reflected a renewed perception of his identity as a Kingdom warrior.

All "warrior material" can be accessed and honed through relationship with Jesus.

Consider this book a war-cry directed at your spirit man, the warrior within. Most of the admirable qualities discussed ahead are already inside of you. Some have been dormant. Others have been underdeveloped, inactive, or even suppressed. Regardless of our present state, we have this assurance: All "warrior material" can be accessed and honed through relationship with God.

I pray by the time you reach the back cover, the warrior within will be commissioned or re-commissioned by our King, Jesus, to have an active role in advancing His Kingdom.

You are a Kingdom Advancer!

You are a Kingdom Warrior!

Believe it!

Heeey!

CHAPTER 1

THE DRIVER
OF PASSION

~ *Nothing great in the world has been accomplished without passion* ~
Georg Wilhelm Friedrich Hegel

One end of our garden hose is connected to the outside water faucet. The other end features a screw-on sprayer called a Water Jet Attachment. This inexpensive and easy-to-use device has been designed to turn an ordinary water hose into a pressure washer.

Water enters the attachment at normal water pressure; it comes out the other end forcefully enough to accomplish any or all of the following tasks:

- Removal of dirt and mold on wood or aluminum siding and concrete foundations
- Washing of automobiles, motorcycles, campers, or boats
- Blasting of weeds and grime from brick and concrete patios, pool decks, and driveways

I liken passion to our jet sprayer. It causes the normal flow of God's love and power within us to be released with force that can bring cleansing, refreshing, and transformation all around us.

> Our level of passion will determine the degree to which the rivers within will bring transformation to those around us.

Passion generates intensity inside, thus converting feelings of appreciation, admiration, interest, compassion, care, and devotion into action-action that touches and changes lives.

Streams of life-transforming water are flowing inside us. Our level of passion will determine the degree to which the rivers within will bring transformation to those around us.

The late Special Forces Lieutenant General, Dhimitrios Christoyiannis, was the commander of my Green Beret unit. He was a Major at the time.

I served under Commander Christoyiannis when he was in his late forties. He was of medium height and weighed about one hundred and thirty pounds. His biceps were the size of most Commandos' wrists. His legs swam inside the pant legs of his trousers. Nothing in his physical appearance or demeanor ever communicated that Dhimitrios Christoyiannis was in command of a Green Beret unit. He, *too*, did not look like warrior material!

Commander Christoyiannis did not speak much; he asked many questions and listened intently without interrupting. However, when he *did* speak, and especially when he addressed his men, the Major spoke with a passion that caused a shift in the atmosphere.

He spoke with authority and a deep commitment to a cause that was bigger than all of us. His voice reflected a tremendous sense of confidence, yet it was always tempered with humility.

> No one can ever over-emphasize the significance of passion in a warrior culture.

His eyes lit up, boring right through us with every gaze. His scrawny limbs, as though energized by electric currents, literally shook. It was as though our commander was on fire!

My comrades and I remember and speak of Major Christoyiannis with the utmost respect and even awe. What we appreciate most was his passion.

No one can ever over-emphasize the significance of passion in a warrior culture. Passion motivates and inspires; it sustains during times of trial and it helps maintain focus; passion combats lethargy, mediocrity, and complacency as it spurs us into action.

Moreover, passion is contagious. Following and serving is exhilarating and meaningful when we follow passionate leaders.

All of us who served under Commander Christoyiannis remember a cold, rainy, wintry evening when we stood in the barracks soccer field, awaiting his orders. It had been a full day of intense training. We were already drenched from the rain. Everyone, including the officers who had conveniently taken cover under a gazebo roof, expected to be dismissed to dry off, eat, and rest.

Major Christoyiannis walked out and stood across from us in the pelting rain. He scanned the troops for a while before speaking (long enough to convict the officers to leave the cover of the gazebo and join us in the rain).

"Commandos," he bellowed, "Rain and cold are not adversaries; they are allies..."

The atmospheric shift was already under way...

"...For they cause our enemies to take cover. They least expect us on nights like this. They are most vulnerable on nights like this. Therefore, I am calling for a night drill, by which we will learn how to take advantage of such *ideal* weather conditions."

Before any under-the-breath mumbling could ensue, the Commander added:

"And I am going *with* you. In fact, I will lead the way. I have been longing for the opportunity!"

Suddenly, soldiers' hairs stood on end. We began to exchange looks of admiration and respect for our commander. Heads began to nod in agreement. Our hearts were inspired to look past our weariness, hunger, and all former expectations to the assignment we had just been given.

Our wet clothes were not as bothersome. We ignored the cold. As one man, we fixed our gaze on our leader, tightened our grips around our rifles, and marched into the night for what turned out to be a very productive drill.

What caused the shift? What changed our disposition? What challenged us to press on and literally "go the extra mile"?

One leader's passion!

Jesus Christ did much more than march a few miles to perform a drill alongside us in the rain. His passion for humanity drove Him from heaven to earth to live among us, reveal the Father's love to us, teach us God's ways, impart His grace, and ultimately sacrifice Himself for us.

Jesus was rejected, mocked, and falsely accused. He was spat upon. He was beaten with men's fists and was scourged by a whip that tore the flesh off His back. He carried His own cross up Golgotha. Soldiers drove nails through His hands and feet. He shed His blood. He gave His life. What passion He demonstrated for you and me!

Passion is an expression of love. God is both the originator and personification of love; thus, He is the source of passion.

Passion is an expression of love. God is both the author and personification of love; thus, He is the original source of passion.

Beloved, let us love one another, for love is of God; and everyone who loves is born of God and knows God. He who does not love does not know God, for God is love.
1 John 4:7-8

Parents passionately protect their children from influences, mindsets, or predators who might try to harm them. Their passionate protectiveness stems from love. Likewise, patriotic soldiers, often sacrificing their very lives, passionately contend for the protection and advancement of the country they love. The sacrifice of Jesus on the cross is the epitome of God's unconditional, passionate love for us.

In this the love of God was manifested toward us, that God has sent His only begotten Son into the world, that we might live through Him.
1 John 4:9

As a result of Christ's sacrifice, and especially His resurrection from the dead, we obtain new life through Him. His love draws us to Himself and then begins to dwell in us. His passion rises up within us and fires up our warrior spirit.

I have had the privilege of serving numerous mission projects, some foreign, some domestic. On every trip there is at least one moment that changes me forever. At those times, God seems to swing a wrecking ball from heaven right through me.

One such moment came on my first trip to Africa. I had joined the president of the International Center for Christian Leadership (ICCL), Dr. Gary Kellner, and a remarkable team of pastors, itinerant ministers, and intercessors to minister among the Massai tribe in Kenya.

We rode buses through small villages and dusty roads. We came face-to-face with brokenness and poverty unlike anything I had ever seen before.

After four years of drought, the Massai people were in desperate need of water, food, and many other commodities we often take for granted. On several occasions, while witnessing the severity of this tribe's condition, I was overwhelmed with emotion. I would walk away from the group for a few minutes so I could bury my face in my hands and weep.

My tears did not stem from pity for the poor in Kenya. Nor was I influenced by a spirit of false humility or guilt for the abundance I have at home.

God had used what I had seen as an invitation to explore yet another fold of His heart, that special place He reserves for the poor. I felt His compassion for the broken, needy, oppressed, underprivileged, rejected, and neglected children of God. As His passion flooded my heart, my emotions peaked and tears naturally flowed.

> All our knowledge, experience, intellect, and reasoning take a back seat, and passion drives us to the front lines of battle.

We are never the same after we receive an impartation of the Father's passion for His children. All our knowledge, experience, intellect, and reasoning take a back seat, and passion drives us to the front lines of battle.

The front-most part of the front lines is reserved for Kingdom warriors, who have a passion to feed the hungry, clothe the naked, heal the sick, house the homeless, parent the orphans, and show God's love and kindness to the oppressed and downtrodden people of the earth.

From the outset of His public ministry, Jesus knew He had been assigned the front-most part of the front lines:

> " *The Spirit of the LORD is upon Me,*
> *because He has anointed Me to preach*
> *the gospel to the poor; He has sent Me to*
> *heal the brokenhearted, to proclaim*
> *liberty to the captives and recovery of*

sight to the blind, to set at liberty those who are oppressed; To proclaim the accept-able year of the LORD."
Luke 4:18-19

Passion is the key qualifier for assignments on the front lines. Skill, training, and experience come with time, but the equipping process cannot even commence unless we have passion.

Passion is the key qualifier for assignments on the front lines. Skill, training, and experience come with time, but the equipping process cannot even commence unless we have passion.

Passion activates, energizes, and sustains our warrior spirit; consequently, we must maintain activities, influences, and relationships that keep our passion burning, especially when we face adversity.

The thirteenth and fourteenth chapters of the Book of Numbers tell the story of twelve spies sent to scope out the land of Canaan and bring back a report to Moses and all the Israelites.

Two of the spies, Joshua and Caleb, had a favorable report. In essence, they said:

"The land is good, just like God told us. Let us advance and conquer Canaan, immediately. We can certainly do this!"

The other ten spies gave a different report:

"The conquest of Canaan is too much for us to handle. The people are too strong; the cities are large and well fortified. The land is not as good as we thought, for 'it devours its inhabitants.' This is way over our heads. We had best stay put and forget about Canaan."

The ten spies' bad report spread fear and unbelief among the Israelites, who began to cry, complain against Moses, and question God's plan.

Joshua and Caleb tried to talk sense into the crowd by insisting the land was good, God was backing up His people, and He was giving them Canaan—all they had to do was follow His directive and invade the land. Joshua and Caleb's attempts failed. The people talked of stoning them.

Then God intervened! He expressed to Moses His anger with the people, and His plans to "...strike them with pestilence and disinherit them" (Numbers 14:12).

Moses interceded on behalf of the people, asking God to reconsider:

> "Pardon the iniquity of this people, I pray, according to the greatness of Your mercy, just as You have forgiven this people, from Egypt even until now."
> Numbers 14:19

God heard Moses' plea and relented from destroying the Israelites; however, He decreed that all the Israelites would die in the wilderness without ever entering the Promise Land:

> *I have pardoned, according to your word; but...all these men who have seen My glory and the signs which I did in Egypt and in the wilderness, and have put Me to the test now these ten times, and have not heeded My voice, they certainly shall not see the land of which I swore to their fathers, nor shall any of those who rejected Me see it.*
> Numbers 14:20-23

Caleb was an exception in God's decree (along with Joshua):

> *But My servant Caleb, because he has a different spirit in him and has followed Me fully, I will bring into the land where he went, and his descendants shall inherit it.*
> Numbers 14:24

What constituted Caleb's "different spirit" was faith in God's promise and a warrior spirit consistently fueled by a passion for the advancement of God's Kingdom.

Caleb was forty years old when he and Joshua stood their ground, insisting they invade Canaan. They barely escaped a stoning by the masses who opposed them, but were the only survivors (along with their households) of the Israelites' desert wanderings.

Forty-five years later, Joshua was in command. God had already used him mightily to lead Israel deeper and deeper into Canaan through war and conquest.

The fortified cities on the hills and mountains—the land of the Anakim giants—remained to be conquered. By virtue of the inhabitants' great physical stature and prowess, as well as their military advantage of possessing the high ground, these cities seemed impenetrable. The task of fighting the uphill battle to conquer them was daunting, to say the least.

One man volunteered for the assignment, Caleb.

Even forty-five years later, Caleb lived for the opportunity to take down the giants and conquer their cities!

First, Caleb refreshed Joshua's memory of the events at Kadesh Barnea in order to establish his credibility for even bringing up the subject.

> *And Caleb the son of Jephunneh the Kenizzite said to him: "You know the word which the LORD said to Moses the man of God concerning you and me in Kadesh Barnea. I was forty years old when Moses the servant of the LORD*

*sent me from Kadesh Barnea to spy out
the land, and I brought back word to him
as it was in my heart. Nevertheless my
brethren who went up with me made the
heart of the people melt, but I wholly
followed the LORD my God.*
Joshua 14:6-8

Then Caleb proceeded to assure his leader that
he was physically capable to handle the task (at
eighty-five!).

*...Now, here I am this day, eighty-five
years old. As yet I am as strong this day
as on the day that Moses sent me; just as
my strength was then, so now is my
strength for war, both for going out and
for coming in.*
Joshua 14:10-11

Finally, Caleb asked Joshua to favor him with
the assignment:

*Now therefore, give me this mountain of
which the LORD spoke in that day; for
you heard in that day how the Anakim
were there, and that the cities were great
and fortified.* Joshua 14:12

Joshua agreed. Caleb successfully waged war
against the Anakim and took possession of their
land.

Caleb's "strength for war" stemmed from his undying passion and strong spirit. Caleb kept his spirit strong by maintaining his passion to possess the high ground for forty-five years. He kept his thoughts focused on God's promises and his assignment.

> Passion in one individual can be catalytic for corporate breakthrough.

Consequently, Caleb's passion led to a blessing for his entire household, his tribe, and all the Israelites, as they were able to take possession of the strategically located fortified cities. Caleb's life demonstrates how passion in one individual can be catalytic for corporate breakthrough.

This principle was also illustrated by a series of events in the life of our middle child. Caleb (not a coincidence) has always been passionate in defending and supporting individuals who are socially rejected and avoided by their peers.

At one of our conferences with our son's teacher, Danielle and I found out Caleb had taken a very strong stand against the attitude and behavior of some students on his bus towards a particular girl.

The girl always sat alone on the bus because no one wanted to befriend her. Worse yet, kids made fun of her, saying she always wore the same clothes, had bad body odor, did not brush her hair, and was messy.

One day, our son approached his teacher during a break and, with tears in his eyes, told her what had been happening to the girl on the bus. Not as a tattle-tale, but with the boldness and resolve of an activist, he emphasized, "This has to stop!"

Some investigation revealed that most of the girl's personal hygiene issues stemmed from a rough upbringing and recent family troubles. Immediately, there was action from the school.

During our conference with the teacher, Danielle and I were informed that our son's stand had resulted in a significant change on the bus and at school. "Everything is different since he spoke up," Caleb's teacher remarked.

She proceeded to tell us that students befriended the girl on the bus and offered to help with her work in class. One of the boys had gone as far as to lay himself prostrate on the ground so the girl could step on him to reach the monkey bars!

Caleb's passion led to transformation on his bus, his classroom, the playground, and most importantly, the life of one underprivileged girl.

How will *your* passion affect your world? What revolution will *you* spawn when you unleash the rivers of love and compassion that flow inside of you?

What moves you? What thoughts cause you to get fired up on the inside? What drives you to dream big, take huge risks, or weep with joy as you see through your mind's eye the victories you and God will win as you co-labor?

We are most effective and productive when we pursue objectives and set goals in areas we are passionate about. Passion causes our interest to be peaked, and our efforts to be fruitful.

I encourage you to take inventory of your heart, even right now. Prayerfully construct a list of the responsibilities, activities, initiatives, plans, causes, and dreams you are most passionate about. Ask the Holy Spirit to help you prioritize them. Then one by one, pursue them with everything in you, and watch how God will use you to impact lives for eternity.

Volumes of books are yet to be written about the amazing feats God will accomplish through your life as you increasingly become a conduit for His passionate love toward humanity.

CHAPTER 2

EVER-INCREASING COURAGE

cour age: *mental or moral strength to venture, persevere, and withstand danger, fear, or difficulty*

~ *Cautious, careful people, always casting about to preserve their reputation and social standing, never can bring about a reform. Those who are really in earnest must be willing to be anything or nothing in the world's estimation, and publicly and privately, in season and out, avow their sympathy with despised and persecuted ideas and their advocates, and bear the consequences.* ~

Susan B. Anthony

~ *Courage is not simply one of the virtues, but the form of every virtue at the testing point.* ~

C.S. Lewis

~ *Courage is not the absence of fear, but rather the judgment that something else is more important than fear.* ~

Ambrose Redmoon

~ *Courage is being scared to death... and saddling up anyway.* ~

John Wayne

Our passion as Kingdom warriors motivates us and spurs us into action; however, passion alone cannot carry us through all the phases of war. Another significant component required for continual advances and sustained victories on life's battlefields is courage.

The quality of courage can never be overrated.

Our need for courage cannot be overstated.

War is dangerous. Warriors are always faced with the possibility of getting hurt or suffering loss. The danger associated with fighting battles, combined with human reasoning and self-preservation, can open the door to fear.

Once fear establishes a foothold in us, it works against us from within to limit us and render us ineffective in carrying out our mission. If we continue to agree with fear, we will eventually assume a neutral or defensive position, and we may cease to live for advancement.

> [Courage] minimizes considerations of risk and danger; instead, courage magnifies the significance of the Cause and the rewards of self-sacrifice.

Courage is absolutely essential for every individual who is determined to fulfill his or her God-given destiny. It minimizes considerations of risk and danger; instead, courage magnifies the significance of the cause and the rewards of self-sacrifice.

Courage does not play as significant a role when there is nothing valuable to obtain or lose. We need courage to fight for the rich spiritual blessings we already possess, as well as everything God makes available to us as we grow in Him.

There are various dimensions or degrees of courage needed, depending on the magnitude of the blessing for which we are contending. The greater the treasure or breakthrough, the greater the dimension of courage required. An encounter in the life of Joshua illustrates this concept:

After Moses died, God gave Joshua the command to lead the people across the Jordan River and into the land He was giving them, Canaan.

God promised Joshua He would be with him, as He was with Moses. God assured Joshua He would grant him victory. Through conquest, Joshua would control a vast territory. Moreover, God promised that no one would prevail against Joshua for the remainder of his life.

That was quite a promise! What leader would not love to have the Almighty God guarantee lasting success at the very outset of his tenure?

God's promise was not unconditional. He had some expectations of Joshua; first and foremost, that he possess strength and courage:

> *"Be strong and courageous, because you will lead these people to inherit the land I swore to their forefathers to give them. Be strong and very courageous."*
> Joshua 1:6-7

When God required strength and courage from Joshua, it was not because Joshua had failed to *show* courage; it was because Joshua would need to *grow* in courage.

God was not admonishing Joshua to be courageous because he lacked courage. Joshua had already been selected as one of Moses' "choice men" (Numbers 11:28); as one of the twelve leaders who were sent to spy out Canaan (Numbers 13:6); and as the leader who would replace Moses:

> *And the LORD said to Moses: "Take Joshua the son of Nun with you, a man in whom is the Spirit, and lay your hand on him; set him before Eleazar the priest and before all the congregation, and inaugurate him in their sight.*
> Numbers 27:18-19

All the positions of responsibility Joshua held, especially that of leading Israel, demanded courage. So when God required strength and courage from Joshua, it was not because Joshua had failed to *show* courage; it was because Joshua would need to *grow* in courage:

> *"Be strong and courageous, **because you will lead these people to inherit the land"** (emphasis mine).*
> Joshua 1:6

The track record of courage that had helped establish Joshua into various positions of leadership would not carry him through the challenges up ahead. When Moses and the Israelites left Egypt, they had to flee. In the desert, they had to follow (a pillar of cloud by day and a pillar of fire by night). To conquer Canaan, they would have to fight; and to fight they would need strength and courage, beginning with the leader.

Leaving Egypt, crossing the Red Sea, and surviving the desert would pale in comparison with what awaited Joshua in Canaan. He would face raging river rapids in flood stage, giants, mighty kings, vast armies, impenetrable walls, and a score of other impossibilities. A new dimension of courage had to be attained.

The level of courage within us has to continually grow in order to meet the increasing demands of our destiny-fulfilling assignments.

We can never draw from courage we may have demonstrated in the past to overcome current or future problems. With each new challenge, we need an increased measure of God's grace. Through grace, we enter into the new dimension of courage for our needed breakthrough.

In other words, we enter new dimensions of courage as a result of having fresh encounters with God. Many times, we experience such courage-building encounters through adversity.

In 1997, Danielle and I spent a week in a series of revival meetings that left us changed forever. We have never been then same since that April week in '97.

Our passion for God increased dramatically. We returned determined to pursue God and seek everything He had for us. We read books about revivalists and the significant works God accomplished through them. With tears in our eyes and an insatiable hunger for more, we often prayed, "God, we want to be on the front seat of revival. Whatever it takes; whatever the cost; we are committed to a move of your Spirit. Give it to us, God!"

In 2006, one year after our installation as pastors of Valley Shore Assembly of God, the Holy Spirit began to move in our church. People began to demonstrate a hunger for prayer and intercession. We continually entered new dimensions of passion and fervency in worship. Salvations increased. Healings and deliverances began to take place. Attendance tripled. Weekly offerings quadrupled. Danielle and I went home every Sunday, saying, "God has heard our prayers. It's happening..."

We started to host monthly revival meetings. We welcomed apostles, prophets, and evangelists, each of whom made significant deposits in our lives. We networked with other pastors, ministries, and churches that had a heart for revival.

Soon, we added more prayer services. We developed an internship program as a foundation for a school of supernatural ministry in the future. We revised our purpose and mission statements, and we defined our core values. Moreover, we began to learn about and establish administrative systems, frameworks, and protocols, by which we would properly steward the blessings of the Lord.

"God heard our prayers. It's happening..."

The word that adequately describes what has taken place at Valley Shore since 2006 is *Transformation* – from "faith to faith" and "glory to glory."

Every time we reached a new level of faith and glory, we pressed in for more of Jesus. God has been faithful to give us the grace to ascend from one level to the next. Growing and ascending is exhilarating and fulfilling; however, we discovered an unpleasant element lurks between each level of faith and glory—adversity!

Back in 1997, when Danielle and I had said, "Whatever it takes; whatever the cost," we had no idea what paying the price could mean.

I choose to leave all the details out. Generally speaking, as a result of the renewal in our church, we have experienced much reproach, persecution, betrayal, derision, loss, and pain. We have been maligned, rejected, accused, and misunderstood by many.

> Adversity will always be present between the levels of faith and glory we graduate from and the new levels we attain.

We have repeatedly come face-to-face with our weaknesses and fears. We have had many opportunities to throw in the towel and look for "safer" assignments. During our darkest moments, when everything that could be shaken was indeed shaken, we refused to quit, and pressed in for fresh encounters with God.

Every time we found the courage to remain steadfast in our passion and calling for revival, a new measure of God's grace was released. At every juncture and with every attack, God intervened on our behalf to help us overcome. Consequently, the blessings of the Lord continue to abound toward us.

Adversity will always be present between the levels of faith and glory we graduate from and the new levels we attain. As we put our trust in Jesus, He gives us the grace to face our trials courageously; thus, we can always remain true to our assignment!

> Wait on the Lord; Be of good courage, and He shall strengthen your heart. Wait, I say on the Lord!
> Psalm 27:14

One of the challenges of the early church was the insistence of some believers that the newly converted and Spirit-filled Gentiles still had to line up with some aspects of the Mosaic Law, including circumcision.

> And certain men came down from Judea and taught the brethren, "Unless you are circumcised according to the custom of Moses, you cannot be saved."
> Acts 15:1

The apostles were very disturbed by the matter. Paul, Barnabas, and a group of other apostles and elders held a council in Jerusalem to resolve the problem.

After various individuals shared their views on the issue, everyone agreed to adopt the recommendations of James, the pastor of the Jerusalem church:

> *Therefore I judge that we should not trouble those from among the Gentiles who are turning to God, but that we write to them to abstain from things polluted by idols, from sexual immorality, from things strangled, and from blood.*
> Acts 15:19-20

The Council determined that a letter be written, communicating the position of the elders and apostles on the matter. The letter was to be hand-delivered by a select group of apostles who would also report on the Jerusalem Council's deliberations.

The way by which the carriers of the letter are introduced to the letter's potential recipients is very significant:

> *It seemed good to us, being assembled with one accord, to send chosen men to you with our beloved Barnabas and Paul, men who have risked their lives for the name of our Lord Jesus Christ.*
> Acts 15:25-26

Our level of commitment to a cause determines the degree of credibility and influence we will have.

Nothing was said about the men's understanding of God's grace having been extended to the Gentiles, their spiritual discernment, their sound doctrine, their theological training, their leadership, or their accomplishments. Only one qualification was given:

These men had risked their lives for Jesus.

The apostles' courage in taking the ultimate risk for the gospel of Christ proved they operated at the highest commitment level; thus, they had the greatest influence and credibility within the Church. Our level of commitment to a cause determines the degree of credibility and influence we will have to uphold the cause.

We are living at a time of accelerated growth and phenomenal increase. God is moving quickly and powerfully in the nations of the earth. We have an amazing opportunity to participate in what will prove to be the greatest revival ever! A courage-fueled willingness for self-sacrifice will be a significant determining factor for the extent of our influence.

Jesus came to the earth to teach and model self-sacrifice. He expects all His disciples to follow His lead.

> From that time Jesus began to show to His disciples that He must go to Jerusalem, and suffer many things from the elders and chief priests and scribes, and be killed, and be raised the third day. Then Peter took Him aside and began to rebuke Him, saying, "Far be it from You,

Lord; this shall not happen to You!"
Matthew 16:21-22

> Our effectiveness as Kingdom warriors depends, in large part, on our willingness to lay our lives on the line and risk everything, continually.

Peter was well-meaning, but he was operating under a mindset of self-preservation, the same mindset that contributed to Peter's denial of Jesus after the Lord's arrest.

Jesus rebuked Peter for his comment, and taught his disciples the opposite of self-preservation: self-sacrifice.

> *Then Jesus said to His disciples, "If anyone desires to come after Me, let him deny himself, and take up his cross, and follow Me. For whoever desires to save his life will lose it, but whoever loses his life for My sake will find it."*
> Matthew 16:24-25

Our effectiveness as Kingdom warriors depends, in large part, on our willingness to lay our lives on the line and risk everything, continually. Once courage takes hold of warriors' hearts, they feel safest when manning their assigned posts on the front lines. They defy danger, take huge risks, and learn to trust God for protection. Consequently, they position themselves for great advancements.

I end this chapter with what I consider some of the bravest words recorded in military history. May this be our attitude as we fight our battles, daily!

Hard pressed on my right.
My center is yielding.
Impossible to maneuver.
Situation excellent. I am attacking.

General Ferdinand Foch at the Battle of the Marne

CHAPTER 3

A LIFETIME
OF TRAINING

~ A man can seldom — very, very, seldom — fight a winning fight against his training; the odds are too heavy. ~

Mark Twain

~ Excellence is an art won by training and habituation. We do not act rightly because we have virtue or excellence, but we rather have those because we have acted rightly. We are what we repeatedly do. Excellence, then, is not an act but a habit. ~

Aristotle

The hardest part of Special Forces training is that it never lets up. From the day a soldier enters boot camp until he is discharged, he trains intensely, continually.

On my last day in uniform, I was awakened by reveille at 6:00 a.m. I ran two miles and performed calisthenics with the rest of the men from my company. I made my bed, organized my belongings, and cleaned my rifle, all in preparation for inspection. Afterwards, I assisted in the cleaning of communal areas. Sure enough, our company was responsible for the toilets that day!

After roll call and inspection, I spent the bulk of the day in training. I do not recall what was taught, but I do remember every instructor pushing me especially hard *because* it was my last day. In the evening, I participated in the setting up and breaking down for dinner.

A courtesy protocol extends exemption from guard duty on soldiers' last night in the barracks. All day long, I had looked forward to a full night's rest, uninterrupted by the dreaded wake-up call for service in the middle of the night.

Shortly before I dozed off, an announcement came over the loudspeakers, summoning me to the officers' quarters. The Captain in charge informed me someone had taken ill. Being the only person without assigned duty for the night, I was ordered to fill in — graveyard shift, nonetheless!

God puts us through a continual training process to teach us the eternal principles that govern His Kingdom.

While standing on an elevated guard post in the early hours of the morning, I reflected on my time in the service. I had experienced many good times, some very challenging times, and constant training, all the way up to the very last moment.

God trains His warriors similarly to the Special Forces. Day by day, experience by experience, "line upon line" and "precept upon precept", God puts us through a continual training process to teach us the eternal principles that govern His Kingdom.

Jesus offered a synoptic view of God's training program when He first approached a group of fishermen who were soon to become His disciples:

> *And as He walked by the Sea of Galilee, He saw Simon and Andrew his brother casting a net into the sea; for they were fishermen. Then Jesus said to them, "Follow Me, and I will make you become fishers of men." They immediately left their nets and followed Him.*
> Mark 1:16-18

In the original Greek text, Jesus' words, "make you to become," are expressed through the word, *poieō.*

Herewith the definition:

> To make, that is to say to form, produce, expressing an action as continued or not yet completed; what one does repeatedly, continually.

In other words, "becoming" fishers of men would require a *process* of training.

Regardless of the level of difficulty, God's training process prepares us for improvement, increase, advancement, and success.

> Training is a means to an end. God is training us for battle, for victory, and ultimately for dominion.

When we perceive seemingly unfavorable circumstances, such as my last-minute guard duty, as part of our training, we are less prone to become frustrated, feel sorry for ourselves, or complain.

Consider the Olympic athlete who steps up to the podium to receive her bouquet of flowers and gold medal. I assure you, while her national anthem is playing and the whole world is watching, the champion is in no way resentful of her training.

She recognizes that the daily workouts, the special diets, the seasons of injury, and the innumerable sacrifices she made over the years paved the way to that glorious moment of victory. I am certain, as the last tear streaks down her cheek at the closing of the anthem; she believes her training was worth it.

Training is a means to an end. God is training us for battle, for victory, and ultimately for dominion. King David understood that principle very well:

> *Blessed be the LORD my Rock,*
> *Who trains my hands for war,*
> *And my fingers for battle*
> Psalm 144:1

Many times, we train for war through processes that do not have anything to do with warfare. Some warrior qualities get developed in us while we are involved in non-warlike activities and environments.

Consider David's life:

Within a very short span of time, David transitioned from being shepherd to becoming a giant-slayer, an officer in Saul's army, and ultimately commander over Israel's men of war (1 Samuel 18:5).

David never enlisted in the army, nor did he receive officer training, yet he rose to a prominent position of military leadership. In his song to the Lord, David praises God as the One who trained him for warfare.

So, where did God train David? Not on a battlefield; more like the sheepfold or the fields where Jesse's sheep grazed. David spent his time at work, worship, and meditation, not soldiery of any kind.

Even the killing of lions and bears does not qualify as warrior training, for it was a rare occurrence. David's *daily* training revolved around fulfilling responsibilities which demanded obedience, faithfulness, diligence, kindness, caring, dependability, courage, selflessness, and wholehearted devotion to God.

David's warfare training may have been unconventional; however, it produced a great warrior, an outstanding general, and arguably the best king Israel ever had.

Moses was destined to become the deliverer of God's people from the bondage of Egypt. His early training took place (ironically) in the palace of Pharaoh, as God had divinely orchestrated his upbringing. Moses was educated in the courts of the very kingdom he raised his staff against a few decades later.

After he killed an Egyptian and ran for his life, Moses entered a different phase of training in the desert, where he tended his father-in-law's sheep. Again, the training was unconventional, but Moses' assignment and especially the impact of that assignment were phenomenal.

The training of another Jew, Daniel, also took place in the courts of an earthly king. After the conquest of Jerusalem, the Chaldean emperor, Nebuchadnezzar, set up an elaborate training program for children of Israelite nobles—"young men in whom there was no blemish, but good-looking, gifted in all wisdom, possessing knowledge and quick to understand" (Daniel 1:2-3).

The king ordered that these young men be taught "the language and literature of the Chaldeans," and that they be granted "a daily provision of the king's delicacies and of the wine which he drank." The training was to last three years, at the end of which time the young men would "serve before the king" (Daniel 1:1-3).

Nebuchadnezzar was training Daniel and his friends to serve in his courts. God was preparing them *through* Nebuchadnezzar's elaborate training program, to follow His ways, hear His voice, refuse to compromise, and trust in Him completely.

Through the resources of a heathen nation, God trained and positioned Daniel for leadership and influence, not only in Nebuchadnezzar's courts, but in the leadership infrastructures of three more world rulers to follow.

We don't always recognize training exercises for what they are. We often label everything that seems adverse as trouble that comes from satan. Daniel and his three friends were undoubtedly under great spiritual attack, as they were orphaned, uprooted from their land, made eunuchs, and forced to serve an ungodly king. Yet, God had a plan to work everything for good and to advance His Kingdom through them.

> Through our past trials and setbacks, God forges in us the faith, character, wisdom, and determination we need for upcoming battles.

God can train us through all circumstances if we are teachable and willing to pay the price. Through our past trials and setbacks, God forges in us the faith, character, wisdom, and determination we need for upcoming battles.

The Apostle Paul said it perfectly:

> *For our light affliction, which is but for a moment, is working for us a far more exceeding and eternal weight of glory,*
> 2 Corinthians 4:17

At some point in their lives, Daniel, Moses, David, and everyone else whose story illustrates this principle, seem to have had a shift in their mindset. The mindset shift enabled them to view potentially debilitating trouble as divinely prescribed training, which positioned them for influence, prominence, wealth, and power.

What causes such a mindset shift?

Encounters with God, due to our attitude of thankfulness.

A heart of thanksgiving filters negative experiences and transforms them into elements of life-empowering training.

Our first home featured a basement, which posed two challenges: First, there was dampness in the air due to the occasional flooding after heavy rains and the household's frequently used washer/dryer; secondly, the plants in the basement rooms always needed watering because our furnace was located there as well. Even during times of near-saturation of the downstairs atmosphere

> A thankful heart extracts heaviness out of the atmosphere of adversity and converts it into the substance that nourishes and strengthens our spirit.

with moisture, the plants were still drying up due to the furnace heat.

Oddly enough, we found a solution for both our problems through a dehumidifier. That amazing appliance "sucked" moisture out of the air and deposited the water molecules into a small bucket, drop by drop. Whenever I emptied the bucket, I dumped the water into the thirsty plants. Our dehumidifier took the unwanted element from the air and turned it into sustenance for our plants.

A thankful heart, especially one that remains thankful through trouble, acts very much like our dehumidifier. It extracts heaviness out of the atmosphere of adversity and converts it into the substance that nourishes and strengthens our spirit.

When life is hard, thankfulness is not a natural expression or emotion; it's a choice. When we choose to thank God through all circumstances, good and bad, we align ourselves with His will for our lives.

Rejoice always, pray without ceasing, in everything give thanks; for this is the will of God in Christ Jesus for you.
1 Thessalonians 1:16-18

Think of a thankful heart as a rope that enables us to climb higher and higher on the mountains of trial and impossibility. Once we reach the top, we can see "the big picture," in which our challenges are truly part of our training for greater conquests.

When we are thankful, teachable, and tuned to God's voice, we obtain valuable training, even through the most menial and seemingly unspiritual tasks.

I receive some of my best training for pastoring a church from my participation in the organic garden on our church property.

Consider for example the simple task of weeding. Weeds are easiest to remove when they are small. If the garden is neglected, weeds will grow and multiply; therefore, much more time and energy must be applied to remove them. Moreover, the removal of large weeds with extensive root systems can disturb and jeopardize the roots of neighboring healthy plants.

It works the same way within a church family. Neglecting or choosing not to address small problems, especially those of a leadership nature, will cost more time, effort, and even resources in the future. It is important to deal with issues before they grow and spread. Even so, the "weeds" must be removed carefully and strategically, so as not to cause an unnecessary disturbance to fruit-bearing programs or individuals within the church.

I obtained another weeding lesson from one of the tools we use for weeding, the stirrup hoe. A metal hoe in the shape of a musical triangle is attached to a wooden handle. The bottom of the triangle digs about an inch or two into the ground as the user pulls the handle toward him or her. In the process, every weed in its path gets pulled up from the root. The stirrup hoe is very effective. It is easiest to use in the areas between fruit-bearing plants.

Some weeds, however, grow right beside the plants we try to preserve. The stirrup hoe may pull up good plants along with weeds; therefore, we cannot use the same tool or tactic with all the weeds in a garden. Sometimes, we just have to get on our hands and knees and carefully extract the unwanted weeds.

Some challenges we face in the Body require the same type of meticulous attention. The tools and methods which have brought resolution in the past may not be appropriate in all similar cases. We often have to seek the Lord for specific strategy and timing.

Everything we do occupationally, socially, or recreationally; every place we visit; everything we learn academically or experientially; and all aspects of our walk with Christ can contribute to our training process as soldiers in the armies of the Lord. What maximizes our capacity for growth and advancement is our desire to learn, combined with our aversion to complacency with what we already know.

In other words, we continue and flourish in God's training regimen for our lives when we recognize that the knowledge and training we have already received cannot sustain us on all battlefields for the remainder of our lives. There's more available through Christ, and we must pursue it!

I wake up every morning aware that God is willing to teach and train me through all my day's experiences. Before I even get out of my bed, I often pray:

> *Show me Your ways, O LORD; teach me*
> *Your paths. Lead me in Your truth and*
> *teach me, for You are the God of my*
> *salvation; on You I wait all the day.*
> Psalm 25:4-5

I encourage you to pray that prayer regularly. Pray it right now! Ask the Lord Jesus to train your hands for war and your fingers to fight. Ask Him to train you for battle, through all life's challenges and trials. And join me in picking up the rope of thanksgiving, and climbing towards the summit of our mountains.

God will always honor and reward our desire to grow, our willingness to learn, and our deliberate choice to be thankful in all things.

Appreciate, endure, and even *enjoy* your training process, being mindful of this eternal truth:

> *He who has begun a good work in you will complete it until the day of Jesus Christ*
> Philippians 1:6

CHAPTER 4

CONQUERING THE FLESH

Every soldier is a product of a manifold training and preparation process. Every aspect of that process hinges on self-discipline.

I have suffered from chronic back pain for years. I have visited many different doctors, physical therapists, and back specialists. I have received various diagnoses; I have followed numerous treatment plans. My primary course of action has been prayer.

My wife and I have prayed for my back intensely from Day One of this trouble. I have gone forward for healing at church services, conferences, and private ministry settings more times than I can possibly remember. I continue to pray and trust the Lord for complete and total healing. He is faithful!

Throughout my journey toward healing and restoration, I have also tried numerous forms of exercise, including walking, rowing, cycling, swimming, yoga, weight-lifting, and even the extreme exercise program, P90X.

After eight years of trial and error, I have found running to be an ideal form of exercise for me. Running loosens and strengthens my back without any negative post-workout effects.

A friend of our family, who is a physical trainer, taught my wife and me how to obtain the maximum benefit from our runs. First, she ran with us for a few days; then she gave each of us a training program.

I maintained my running regimen for a few months; then winter settled over New England, making it very difficult to run outside. Though we own a treadmill, I convinced myself "it's not the same," and I eventually abandoned my running routine.

By springtime the following year, my back had regressed to the point of spasms and excruciating pain. Not only had I lost my gains from several months of running, I ended up in the worse condition ever.

Following an international ministry trip, which had very adverse effects on my back, I went back to my physical trainer crying, "help!"

To my utter disbelief, my trainer did not massage my back or apply ultrasound to relieve the pain. She took me for a run! Each step brought excruciating pain. I was convinced I would collapse at any moment.

We ran about a mile. My trainer talked to me the entire time, teaching me various principles of motion. She assured me I would not only survive the run, but would actually feel much better afterwards. She was right. By the time we returned, all my pain was gone!

As I drove home that morning, I realized that until God healed my back, running was not optional, but mandatory. If I were to have a chance to fulfill my obligations to my family, enjoy playtime with my children, work around the yard, and carry out my responsibilities as a minister of the gospel, I would need a healthy back. To have a healthy back, I would need to run; and to run, I would have to exercise self-discipline.

> Maximizing our potential by utilizing our gifts, abilities, and experiences relies heavily on our willingness to discipline our body and mind.

Since that morning, I have been running at least four times a week. Self-discipline goes beyond the run itself. It involves carving out the time to exercise, eating appropriate meals, staying hydrated, laying out running clothes before bedtime in order not to wake everyone up early the next morning, and maintaining a daily stretch routine to keep my muscles loose.

I offer my story to illustrate a very important fact:

Maximizing our potential by utilizing our gifts, abilities, and experiences relies heavily on our willingness to discipline our body and mind.

One of the first objectives of military training is to teach soldiers self-discipline because it is the foundation of every aspect of military life. Regardless of branch, rank, experience, skill, or function, every component of a warrior's life demands a degree of self-discipline.

> Regardless of branch, rank, experience, skill, or function, every component of a warrior's life demands a degree of self-discipline.

I have vivid memories of my days of training in explosives and demolition. The officer who taught our group started every session with the following sobering statement:

> *In explosives/demolition, your first mistake can very well be your last!*

Then, drawing from all twenty-five years of his experience on the field, he inspected us head-to-toe, directing his full attention to every minute detail of our attire and equipment.

Even the smallest omission or oversight by one soldier cost him and the rest of the group dearly. As the group grunted, huffed, and puffed through a litany of undesirable calisthenics, our instructor would add:

> *In explosives/demolition, your partner's first mistake can very well claim your life as well.*

Not only were we trained to be fully prepared as individuals, we also had to learn to spot the errors and inconsistencies of our comrades. Therefore, our individual and collective preparation for class began long before class time, oftentimes the night before.

We were not even allowed to come near explosives or explosive devices, much less use them, until our instructors were fully convinced every member of the class had demonstrated self-discipline through meticulous attention to detail.

Some of the principles from demolition training apply to our lives as Kingdom-advancing warriors. The Apostle Paul states we have access to weapons far more powerful than dynamite, TNT, or C4:

> *For the weapons of our warfare are not carnal but mighty in God for pulling down strongholds, casting down arguments and every high thing that exalts itself against the knowledge of God, bringing every thought into captivity to the obedience of Christ*
> 2 Corinthians 10:4-5

In order to respect and effectively use such heavenly weapons, we must bring our bodies and minds under the authority of our spirit, and our spirit under the authority of God, the Holy Spirit.

The more disciplined we become, the more "weapons" God will entrust to us. Our level of self-discipline depends on our willingness and ability to live in the Spirit, instead of the flesh. That means our own spirit must take charge over our flesh, and bring our entire being into alignment with the will, purposes, and ways of God.

> Our effectiveness on the global battlefield is contingent upon victory in the battles between our flesh and the Spirit.

Our effectiveness on the global battlefield is contingent upon victory in the battles between our flesh and the Spirit:

> *I say then: Walk in the Spirit, and you shall not fulfill the lust of the flesh. For the flesh lusts against the Spirit and the Spirit against the flesh; and these are contrary to one another, so that you do not do the things that you wish.*
> Galatians 5:16-17

The very writing of this book is demanding an added measure of discipline in my own life. While working on *Warrior Material*, I have numerous family, ministerial, and social responsibilities to attend to.

My flesh tries to convince me I do not have time to write. My spirit, which is yielded to the Holy Spirit, who gave me this assignment, makes a conscious decision daily, that God will help me *make* time. My spirit outranks my flesh and therefore, it frees me from self-limiting thoughts so I can keep writing.

I am motivated by my desire to be found faithful with the current assignment so God will entrust me with greater revelation, insight, and might for future missions. I discipline my flesh to obey my spirit so I won't get stuck or backtrack, and consequently miss out on advancing from one level of significance to another. In the words of Paul:

> *And everyone who competes for the prize is temperate in all things. Now they do it to obtain a perishable crown, but we for an imperishable crown. Therefore I run thus: not with uncertainty. Thus I fight: not as one who beats the air. But I discipline my body and bring it into subjection, lest, when I have preached to others, I myself should become disqualified.*
> 1 Corinthians 9:26-27

If self-discipline is a two-sided coin, on one side we have the God-honoring, Kingdom-advancing things we must press towards by disciplining our spirit to rule over our flesh. On the other side of the same coin are the God-honoring, Kingdom-advancing things we must leave alone, simply because they have not been assigned to us. It takes as much, if not more, discipline *not* to

> It takes as much, if not more, discipline *not* to pursue some objectives as it does to see others to fruition.

pursue some objectives as it does to see others to fruition.

Think of it as the challenge shoppers in most countries of the western world face at grocery stores. The racks are filled with well-marketed, strategically-stacked products that shout, "Take *me!*" The cereal aisle is my own personal nemesis in that it offers scores of beautifully-colored boxes, full of sugar-loaded delicacies, many times with a "Special Toy" inside!

If it were not for my wife's list to keep me on track, I would easily succumb to the temptations posed throughout the store. I must focus on the items I have been assigned to purchase and avoid the rest; and that requires a degree of self-discipline.

Our opportunities for involvement or participation in Kingdom-advancing projects are many; however, our time is always limited. If we are to stay our course and fulfill our purpose, we must be able to maintain focus on specific assignments for each time and season.

Danielle and I are blessed to be surrounded by a staff and church family comprised of passionate, devoted, industrious, creative, and visionary individuals. God has also gifted us with many Kingdom-advancing ministerial friends, each of whom is continually dreaming big, working hard, sowing liberally, and networking effectively within the Body of Christ. Consequently, we are frequently presented with opportunities to help launch initiatives, participate in events, and form alliances.

Every opportunity is fascinating to us, yet Danielle and I recognize we cannot participate in everything that is made available. We know that being involved in too many pursuits, especially those which are not assigned to us for that specific time or season, can cause misalignment of our priorities. Therefore, as individuals and as a couple, we have developed the discipline of evaluating ministry opportunities by asking the following questions:

- Does God want us to do this?
- Does He want us to do this right now?
- How would our participation in this venture, initiative, partnership or alliance contribute toward the fulfillment of our destiny?
- What is required and expected of us in terms of time, energy, and resources?
- Are we able to participate and still properly balance our priorities?
- Does pride, the opinions of men, or selfish ambition have even the slightest input in our decision?

Over the last few years, we have turned down many opportunities for Christian service, even invitations for ministry due to our commitment to our three children. There is no preaching engagement, social function, or ministerial responsibility that my wife and I value above our presence at our children's ball games or school performances.

Our church family and all our close confidants have heard us make the following statement:

"We do not put ministry before family, and we do not put family before ministry. Family *is* our ministry. If something has to give, it will be the ministry."

Our friends commend us and the church applauds us for our stand; however, I must be honest to admit we are often tempted to deviate from the standard we have set. At times, we have failed. Our level of success in being true to our commitment is, in large part, dependent upon the discipline to keep our eyes and hands only on what has been assigned to us.

Self-discipline may be daunting at first; however, there comes a tipping point in warriors' lives when they get comfortable with, and even yearn for, the discipline they may have resisted initially. The scale is tipped by the rewards of self-discipline.

As a Green Beret in explosives/demolitions, I was rewarded by being included in thrilling, unforgettable missions involving explosives. For Danielle and I, the reward for honoring priorities is a healthy family environment in which our children blossom in the things of God, without any resentment for our commitment to the ministry.

In every case, the rewards we receive far exceed the efforts we exert or the price we pay.

If you find yourself lacking self-discipline in any area, you have an opportunity right now to make a commitment to God, yourself, and anyone else necessary that you will improve.

If any wrong has been done to others, simply ask forgiveness and be at peace. Then set goals, establish standards, and develop tactics to be more disciplined. I am confident you will see positive results quickly. Once you begin to receive rewards, it will become easier to maintain your disciplines.

Try it. Begin to make those changes now!

CHAPTER 5

CHAIN OF COMMAND

There is a direct correlation between submission to authority and the level of authority we obtain. The more we yield to authority, the more authority we will be granted.

A kingdom is a realm where a king or ruler reigns. Kingdoms advance and grow through alliance and/or conquest—the seizing of territory. The maintenance of a kingdom's existing realm and its expansion into new areas depends upon leaders' and subjects' attitudes and behaviors within their kingdom's established systems of governance.

God's Kingdom is one of order. Everything and everyone has a proper place, a proper function, and a proper mode of operation. Thus, the Kingdom of God operates according to divinely established systems of headship and rulership—authority structures.

Pastor Andy Stanley has coined the phrase, "systems create behaviors." The activities, practices, and mindsets of people within a certain organization or domain are strongly influenced by the systems that are in place.

For instance, at the close of every service in our church, we offer prayer for anyone who desires to receive. When the announcement is made that the altar area is open for prayer, several things take place, almost automatically.

> Systems help establish order, which in turn enables us to attain and sustain growth.

Individuals who are scheduled to serve come forward, face the congregation, and form several teams of two across the front. Individuals who want prayer get out of their seats and begin to move toward the teams in position. The rest of the folks either remain in their seats to intercede or they begin to exit the building, quietly.

When they minister, prayer workers generally follow the pattern or system that has been established through courses we offer on healing, deliverance, and the prophetic. Of course, we are always willing to follow the Holy Spirit in any deviations from our pattern; however, we have learned that following a system when praying for folks better equips us to honor the presence of the Lord and properly exercise spiritual gifts.

Generally, the more experienced person on the team of two is the team leader. He/she is accountable to our head intercessor, and ultimately the pastoral leadership of our church.

Systems help establish order, which in turn enables us to attain and sustain growth. At the end of our services, our congregation "behaves" according to the system we have developed.

Without the system, we would have chaos.

Yes, we learned this the hard way!

When the Spirit first began moving in our midst, many well-meaning, passionate, and anointed believers, some of whom were first-time visitors, were eager to lay hands on folks and see God move. Their motives were pure; however, in the absence of a system, everyone did what he/she thought was best. Their best was not always *the* best for the integrity of our ministry.

Some had a tendency to pray very loudly; others softly. Some barely touched people's foreheads while praying; others were more *forceful* in the laying on of hands. One brother, during his first visit, began to pray for a young lady right in the middle of a service, and then promptly asked her to go out with him. Needless to say, within a couple of weeks, we were at the drawing board to establish systems.

I wholeheartedly agree with Andy Stanley — systems create behaviors!

Jesus rules and reigns in His Kingdom through God's system of delegated authority. At the pinnacle of the system is God, the Father. As the One who existed before everyone and everything; the One who made everything that exists, and who has complete power, control, and authority over the Universe, God reigns supreme.

God commands all the honor and respect we could possibly bestow on Him, and He deserves all the glory.

I am uncomfortable when our Heavenly Father is flippantly referred to as the *"Man upstairs,"* or when I hear remarks such as, "When I get up to heaven, I have some serious questions for the *Big Guy."*

I am not offended by such comments because I recognize they often stem from hurt or ignorance; ultimately, from an improper understanding of God as the ultimate Ruler over heaven and earth.

When we stand before Him, we will not be telling *Him* anything, nor will we be questioning God or demanding answers from Him. The only thing coming out of our mouths will be praise. We will be joining the elders, the four living creatures, the angels, and all the saints to cry:

> *"Holy, holy, holy, Lord God Almighty, Who was and is and is to come!" "You are worthy, O Lord, to receive glory and honor and power; For You created all things, and by Your will they exist and were created."*
> Revelation 4:8, 11

God accomplishes much of His work on the earth by delegating authority to people, as He pleases.

Submission to God's authority and the authority figures he places over our lives is imperative in obtaining and properly exercising authority.

I have yet to meet a successful person who consistently disrespects authority. When I taught seventh and eighth graders in a Christian school, I observed that the best students, athletes, and young leaders were those who properly submitted to the authority of their parents, teachers, school administrators, and pastors.

On the other hand, a common denominator between students who were academically or socially troubled was disrespect for parental, school, and/or church authority. Troubled students' problems rarely stemmed from natural limitations or special needs. They may very well have been brighter, more talented, and more charismatic than others, but they always ended up lagging behind or getting disciplined because of their bad attitude.

Unless there is repentance and transformation from within, seeds of rebellion at the elementary or middle school level will undoubtedly give root to much more serious cases of insubordination in students' lives thereafter. One of the worst effects of resistance and rebellion against authority is self-imposed limitation, which ultimately hinders people from maximizing their Kingdom-advancing potential.

Kingdom warriors' training and effectiveness as Kingdom-advancers peaks during seasons of peace, which are often the direct result of honoring God's authority system.

On the positive side, when we choose to operate within His authority structures, God ensures our growth, safety, and wellbeing, and we live in peace with God and one another.

The best time to train for war is peace time. Kingdom warriors' training and effectiveness as Kingdom-advancers peaks during seasons of peace, which are often the direct result of honoring God's authority system.

Ephesians 6:10-19 has always been a well-quoted portion of Scripture dealing with the subject of spiritual warfare — the type of warfare all of us are engaged in, continually.

The Apostle Paul exhorts believers at Ephesus, and ultimately all believers, to recognize "we do not wrestle against flesh and blood, but against principalities, against powers, against the rulers of the darkness of this age, against spiritual hosts of wickedness in the heavenly places" (verse 12). Hence, we are admonished to "take up the whole armor of God, that [we] may be able to withstand in the evil day, and having done all, to stand."

The armor of God is comprised of the belt of

truth, "the breastplate of righteousness," shoes of "the preparation of the gospel of peace," a "shield of faith," a "helmet of salvation," and "the sword of the Spirit, which is the word of God." (Ephesians 6:13-17)

This portion on spiritual warfare interestingly begins with the word, "finally:"

> **Finally**, *my brethren, be strong in the Lord and in the power of His might.* Ephesians 6:10 (emphasis mine)

The word, "finally," implies a connection between what was communicated earlier with what follows next. What Paul communicated earlier (the latter part of Chapter 5 and the first nine verses of Chapter 6) emphasizes the significance of adhering to God's authority structures.

First, Paul addresses husbands and wives:

> *Wives submit unto your husbands as to the Lord. For the husband is the head of the wife as Christ is the head of the church, his body, of which he is the Savior. Husbands, love your wives, just as Christ loved the church and gave himself up for her...husbands ought to love their wives as their own bodies.* Ephesians 5:22-25, 28

The children are next:

> *Children, obey your parents in the Lord,*
> *for this is right. Honor your father and*
> *mother — which is the first*
> *commandment with a promise — "that it*
> *may go well with you and that you may*
> *enjoy long life on the earth."*
> Ephesians 6:1-4

Then servants:

> *Bondservants, be obedient to those who*
> *are your masters according to the flesh,*
> *with fear and trembling, in sincerity of*
> *heart, as to Christ; not with eyeservice,*
> *as men-pleasers, but as bondservants of*
> *Christ, doing the will of God from the*
> *heart, with goodwill doing service, as to*
> *the Lord, and not to men.*
> Ephesians 6:5-7

And masters:

> *And you, masters, do the same things to*
> *them, giving up threatening, knowing*
> *that your own Master also is in heaven,*
> *and there is no partiality with Him.*
> Ephesians 6:9

The progression of these passages indicates that proper order must be established through submission to authority, and *then* we can obtain the armor, weapons, and training to wage warfare and "be strong in the Lord and in the power of His might."

> A prerequisite for effectively waging warfare against principalities and powers is proper submission to authority, at every level of God's governmental structure.

In other words, a prerequisite for effectively waging warfare against principalities and powers is proper submission to authority, at every level of God's governmental structure.

Authority is, by definition, the right to have control over something or someone; the right to have control over private property, an organization, an establishment, or a group of people.

> Through honoring and submitting to the authority of others, we position ourselves to receive and exercise authority ourselves.

In order to obtain divine authority, we must first walk *under* authority. Through honoring and submitting to the authority of others, we position ourselves to receive and exercise authority.

Jesus set the church up for headship; for dominion; to have power and influence in this world. In order to exercise the authority we have been given over all things, we have to properly position ourselves under God at all times.

Outside of God's ordained system of authority and His ordained headship, the church *cannot* be revived. God will not keep adding newborn babies into Houses that are out of order.

In the United States, before a family can adopt a child, governing authorities take a very close and thorough look at the family. They want to know if the parents and other family members will foster an appropriate atmosphere for adoption through love, support, care, and provision, protection, etc.

God is the same way. He is not an irresponsible Father.

The ministry of Jesus was effective, because He spoke, prayed, exhorted, and rebuked with authority.

> *The people were astonished at his doctrine, for He taught them as one having authority, and not as the scribes.*
> Matthew 7:28-29

> *What thing is this? What new doctrine is this? For with authority He commands even the unclean spirits and they do obey Him.*
> Mark 1:27

Jesus perfectly submitted Himself to governmental, parental, and ecclesiastical authority figures and structures; therefore, He lived and operated with great authority. Moreover, the Lord released His authority to others.

> *"He called His twelve disciples together and gave them power and authority over all devils, and to cure diseases. And He sent them to preach the kingdom of God and to heal the sick."*
> Luke 9:1-2

Christ's submission and obedience made a way for His disciples to access high levels of authority when they were sent out to minister. As long as they were yielded and submissive to the authority of their Lord, the disciples continually grew in favor, power, gifting, understanding, and authority.

As Jesus' disciples today, we have the same responsibility and opportunity as the twelve original disciples. We have a mandate to fulfill the Great Commission by releasing the Kingdom of God in every corner of the Earth. God's authority and power are available to us. May we learn to work within and honor his authority structures so we can maximize the impact of our ministry and life!

CHAPTER 6

A HEART TO HONOR

The giving and receiving of honor depends more on actions than feelings or words.

The concept of honor is tightly woven into the fabric of every military organization around the world. The word "honor" is featured in military unit mottos from several nations:

"For King, Country, and the Honor of the Flag" Royal Norwegian Navy

"Prestige and Honor Everywhere" Indian Regiment of Artillery

"Honor and Fatherland" French Army

"Honor, Fatherland, Valor, Discipline" French Navy

"Honor and Fidelity" U.S. 65 Infantry Regiment

"Honor and Courage" U.S. 8th Cavalry Regiment

"Duty, Honor, Country" United States Military Academy

Honor is also one of the core values for the United States Marine, Army, and Navy Corps.

> The degree of honor we bestow is directly related to the value we ascribe.

Every warrior culture trains and expects soldiers to live honorably themselves, and to properly bestow honor to their superiors and fellow soldiers.

In Kingdom warrior culture, the ultimate honor belongs to God; and to honor *Him*, we must follow the guidelines for giving honor as they are set forth in God's Word.

In the Greek language, "to honor" means "*to praise or to revere.*" It comes from a root word which means "*valuable.*"

Honor builds up inside our hearts as we develop an appreciation for the value of something or someone. The degree of honor we bestow is directly related to the value we ascribe.

Most marketable products or services have two forms of value ascribed to them:

- The value to the consumer or the market in general, i.e., what others are willing to pay or do to obtain the product or service.
- The value to the creator, inventor, or designer that birthed and/or developed the service or product.

It is extremely rare for an inventor or a designer to value his/her product or service less than the market does. In most cases, the opposite occurs. Markets lower the value of products and services to make them more appealing or affordable.

I enjoy the odd hobby of collecting marbles. I have been collecting for more than a decade. Some collectors' marbles are very rare and valuable. In order to preserve such marbles' ever-increasing value, collectors have to find ways to keep their marbles from rubbing against one another.

We use various containers to carry and display our most rare marbles. Foam-lined pistol cases, Styrofoam boxes, padded cigar boxes, or jewelry boxes are often used.

A few years ago, I developed a hinged wooden marble display box with felt-lined recessed holes. I used fine exotic woods and brass hardware. I applied twelve coats of finish on each box. During the span of six months, I produced eleven boxes.

I put my creations up for sale at the Annual New England Marble Show. Though everyone who saw them commented the boxes were well-made, beautiful, and practical, I returned home with all eleven boxes — not one of them sold!

My creations failed to sell because they were very expensive. The price I had set for each box reflected the value I, the maker of the product, had ascribed to my creation. When I reduced the price a few months later, the boxes sold rather quickly.

God, the Creator of all things, always ascribes a higher value to His creation than we do, especially when it comes to human beings, who are created in His image and likeness.

As in the case of passion, honor originates from God:

> *Yours is the kingdom, O LORD,*
> *And You are exalted as head over all.*
> *Both riches and honor come from You,*
> *And You reign over all.*
> 1 Chronicles 29:11-12

God established honor, and entrusted humans with the responsibility of sharing it. In other words, honor comes *from* God through *us*.

> Our worth to God is not determined by our abilities, possessions, accomplishments, or social standing, but on what we carry on the inside.

Having a heart to properly honor people is contingent upon our alignment with God's value system. When, through our fellowship with God, we get a hold of how precious each and every individual is to Him, we will properly "give honor to whom honor is due."

There is a difference between *having* things of value and *being* valuable. Our worth to God is not determined by our abilities, possessions, accomplishments, or social standing, but on what we carry on the inside. God ascribes value to His children based on what He, our Father, has deposited in each of us.

When John the Baptist was asked who he was, he replied:

> *I am the voice of one crying in the wilderness...*
> John 1:23

John the Baptist didn't just *have* a voice; he *was* the voice. John's entire life, not just his occupation or ministry, was dedicated to the preparation of his generation to receive Jesus, the Messiah.

When Jesus honored John before the multitudes, saying, "Among those born of women there has not risen one greater than John the Baptist" (Matthew 11:11), He was valuing John for who he was as a person, not what he had accomplished.

One of my favorite biblical accounts, portraying the Father's value for the people He created, is found in the book of Jonah.

God called Jonah to preach a message of repentance at Nineveh, the capital of the Assyrian Empire:

> *Arise, go to Nineveh, that great city, and cry out against it; for their wickedness has come up before Me.*
> Jonah 1:2

Jonah tried to escape from the assignment by boarding a ship heading in the opposite direction. A violent storm on the high seas, being thrown overboard by desperate sailors, and a "great fish," which "the Lord had prepared," caused Jonah to reconsider.

After three days in the belly of the fish, Jonah had repented for his disobedience, had recommitted his life to God's purposes, and was "vomited" by the fish back onto dry land. When God called for Nineveh again, Jonah complied:

> *So Jonah arose and went to Nineveh,*
> *according to the word of the LORD...*
> *Then he cried out and said, "Yet forty*
> *days, and Nineveh shall be overthrown!"*
> Jonah 3:3, 4

The results from Jonah's ministry were truly remarkable. Nineveh responded with immediate, widespread conviction and repentance:

> *So the people of Nineveh believed God,*
> *proclaimed a fast, and put on sackcloth,*
> *from the greatest to the least of them.*
> Jonah 3:5

Even the king of the land put aside his royal apparel, covered himself with sackcloth and ashes, and issued the following decree throughout the city:

Let neither man nor beast, herd nor flock, taste anything; do not let them eat, or drink water. But let man and beast be covered with sackcloth, and cry mightily to God; yes, let every one turn from his evil way and from the violence that is in his hands. Who can tell if God will turn and relent, and turn away from His fierce anger, so that we may not perish?
Jonah 3:7-9

When God saw the sincere turnaround in the hearts and lives of the Ninevites, He "relented from the disaster that He had said He would bring upon them, and He did not do it." (Jonah 3:10)

Every preacher I have ever known would have rejoiced with such a great conclusion to the "Nineveh Revival." Jonah didn't; instead, he was "exceedingly" displeased "and he became angry" (Jonah 4:1). A few verses later, we find him so upset that he is asking God to take his very life.

Why?

Jonah never understood how serious God was about sparing Nineveh. He went to the city and preached to the people out of obedience, but not out of appreciation or love for God's created beings. Jonah did not appreciate the value God ascribed to the Ninevites.

The Lord proceeded to bring alignment to Jonah through an illustration out of nature. God

> Judgment inhibits our ability to properly assess value.

created a plant which grew tall enough to provide Jonah with shelter from the desert sun. Then God prepared a worm which caused the plant to wither. Jonah consequently lost his shade...and his cool (no pun intended).

> *Then he wished death for himself, and said, "It is better for me to die than to live."*
> Jonah 4:8

God responded to Jonah's pouting with the following words:

> *"You have had pity on the plant for which you have not labored, nor made it grow, which came up in a night and perished in a night. And should I not pity Nineveh, that great city, in which are more than one hundred and twenty thousand persons who cannot discern between their right hand and their left — and much livestock?"*
> Jonah 4:10-11

What caused Jonah to devalue or undervalue the Ninevites was judgment. Judgment inhibits our ability to properly assess value. God saw the Ninevites for who He created them to be, not for who they were in their wrongdoing. God's love and mercy for His valuable creation "triumphed over judgment," and that is why He relented from destroying them.

> The value we have for people, and the degree to which we honor them, will determine the depth of the relationship we can establish with them, and the extent to which we will impact their lives.

When we obtain proper understanding of and respect for God's value system, we have a heart to honor. The value we have for people, and the degree to which we honor them, will determine the depth of the relationship we can establish with them, and the extent to which we will impact their lives.

From God's perspective, the word "honor" is not a noun; it is an action verb. Honoring one another requires deliberate action, not just warm feelings and kind words.

The first biblical mention of honor as a command from God is the fifth commandment:

> *Honor your father and your mother, that your days may be long upon the land which the LORD your God is giving you.*
> Exodus 20:12

In his letters to Timothy, Paul admonished his young protégé to honor widows (1 Timothy 5:3), honor elders with double honor (1 Timothy 5:17), and honor masters (1 Timothy 6:1). Peter exhorts husbands to give honor to their wives (1 Peter

3:17). Also consider Paul's words to the church in Rome:

> *Be kindly affectionate to one another with brotherly love, in honor giving preference to one another.*
> Romans 12:10

In each case, honor requires action. Parents are honored through obedience, demonstrations of love, and acts of service. Widows are honored through provision for their needs and respect within the Body.

In the context of Paul's admonition to Timothy, elders are honored by being compensated well. Masters are honored through excellent and honest service. Wives are honored as their husbands respect, praise, provide, and protect them.

Giving preference to one another also requires deliberate choice and motion. We take a seat and let someone else stand in the spotlight. We give up our turn; we share our resources; we promote others more than ourselves.

At every governmental, social, and relational level, honor is best expressed through action.

At every governmental, social, and relational level, honor is best expressed through action.

On a sleepless night, the Persian King, Ahasuerus, had someone read to him from the book where the chronicles of his kingdom were recorded. An account was read of the assassination plot against the king by two of his eunuchs, Teresh and Bigthana. The account stated that a Jew by the name of Mordecai had uncovered the plot and had promptly reported it to Queen Esther, thus saving the king's life.

Upon hearing of the incident, King Ahasuerus inquired:

> *What honor or dignity has been bestowed on Mordecai for this? And the king's servants who attended him said, "Nothing has been done for him."*
> Esther 6:3

King Ahasuerus was the highest governing authority over a vast and powerful kingdom, namely, the Persian Empire. He answered to no one, for he was the most prominent figure in his kingdom. And yet, upon hearing the account of the folded assassination plot, Ahasuerus' conscience bothered him because nothing had been *done* to honor the man who had saved his life.

In other words, as far as King Ahasuerus was concerned, merely knowing about Mordecai's timely intervention, having gratitude in his heart, and maintaining a written record of the incident did not adequately honor Mordecai. Something had to be *done*.

As a congregation, we are always working to improve in the area of giving honor. We are especially mindful to honor and bless individuals whose service in the Body remains hidden from public view.

My heart is always full of gratitude toward these folks, and I do my best to express my personal appreciation for their work. However, if I truly want to *honor* them, I must take action. I have to plan and execute initiatives which will direct the attention and affection of an entire congregation toward those who selflessly and consistently serve us.

We are also very deliberate about honoring the apostles, prophets, pastors, evangelists, and teachers God sends us. Through hospitality, gifts, honorariums, and the kindness of a grateful congregation, we express honor toward these precious friends who partner with us to establish a church of power and glory.

One of our fathers, Pastor Jan Nel, has said, "The measure of honor you commit to in receiving God's servants will determine the magnitude of the deposit God will make in the House through them."

It is true! Our guests' ministry has a powerful and widespread impact as we properly honor them.

Failing to honor God's servants will have the opposite effect. At one point during his ministry, Jesus returned to his hometown of Nazareth. He taught in the synagogue and people were astonished, saying:

> *Where did this Man get this wisdom and these mighty works? Is this not the carpenter's son? Is not His mother called Mary? And His brothers James, Joses, Simon, and Judas? And His sisters, are they not all with us? Where then did this Man get all these things?"*
> Matthew 13: 54-55

The people's familiarity with Christ as a "son of Nazareth" became a stumbling block for them. They refused to recognize and honor His anointing, gifts, and purpose; instead, "they were offended at Him" (verse 57). Consequently, Nazareth missed out on the great things Jesus desired to accomplish there:

> *But Jesus said to them, "A prophet is not without honor except in his own country and in his own house." Now He did not do many mighty works there because of their unbelief.*
> Matthew 13:58

The last biblical reference exhorting us *to honor* is found in 1 Peter, Chapter 2:

For this is the will of God, that by doing good you may put to silence the ignorance of foolish men — as free, yet not using liberty as a cloak for vice, but as bondservants of God. Honor all people. Love the brotherhood. Fear God. Honor the king.
1 Peter 2:15-17

Through these words, especially the admonition to honor the king, Peter modeled the highest level of honor — honor for those who act dishonorably toward us.

By honoring our critics or enemies, we model Christ's unconditional love and forgiveness; and thus, we further align ourselves with God's perfect will for our lives.

Peter wrote his first letter between the years 62 AD and 64 AD. The "king" at the time was Nero, a cruel and mentally unstable Roman emperor who was ultimately responsible for the torture and murder of many Christians. Peter himself was executed on Nero's watch, soon after he wrote this letter. Yet, Peter did not tell believers merely to tolerate the king or to do their best to avoid him until his time was up — Peter said, "Honor him"!

By honoring our critics or enemies, we model Christ's unconditional love and forgiveness; and thus, we further align ourselves with God's perfect will for our lives.

Every time we are hurt by the actions and words of others, we must draw closer to the Lord and ask for the grace to completely forgive and release the perpetrators. Once love and forgiveness floods our hearts, we then turn the tables on the enemy by blessing and honoring those who hurt us.

At any given moment, our church is supporting individuals or ministries who have openly judged or criticized us. We do not bless our enemies to prove a point or to feel good about ourselves. We do it because the love of God has been shed abroad in our hearts and we truly desire to share His love with all people. In fact, it is our *enemies* who need His love the most!

Some of our greatest breakthroughs, which always translate as transformed lives through the resurrection power of Jesus, have come after we have deliberately and joyfully honored those who dishonored us.

I encourage you to wholeheartedly honor individuals who are opposed to you and those who have deliberately hurt you. I guarantee you will experience a significant difference on the inside. More importantly, the Father will be pleased and the example and Name of Jesus will be honored.

As we value and honor our family members, friends, the people who serve us, governmental authorities, or our enemies, let us remember God's everlasting promise:

> *Those who honor Me I will honor...*
> 1 Samuel 2:30

May God richly reward you with peace and a greater revelation of His love as you bless and honor everyone!

CHAPTER 7

FIGHT TO THE FINISH

~ Never give in — never, never, never, never, in nothing great or small, large or petty, never give in...never yield to force; never yield to the apparently overwhelming might of the enemy. ~

Winston Churchill

One of my concerns with today's society is that we are becoming less and less uncomfortable with quitting.

Some of our mindsets, cultural norms, and socioeconomic infrastructures have made it easier than ever before for people to give up on life's pursuits, even life itself. Students drop out of school, employees walk off their jobs, couples end their marriages, church members leave their churches, and dreamers abandon their dreams, often without even putting up a fight against the challenges they face.

Phrases such as, "I quit," "I give up," "I'm starting over," or "I want out," are used frequently without much thought for the consequences. During a time of economic recession, the United States Congress deliberated for months to find solutions and remedies for various financial problems. One result from their efforts was the enactment of a series of initiatives called, "bail-outs." Since then, bail-outs seem more acceptable, in more areas than just finances.

> Language makes a difference; and the language we use now, especially since the "bail-outs", makes quitting more acceptable.

I am not speaking for or against the policies enacted by the US Congress; but I *am* concerned about the concept of "bail-outs" being encouraged by the highest legislative body in the land.

The language we use influences our mindsets. In different units of the military, especially the Special Forces, those who feel they cannot complete the training yell out a drop-out phrase such as Drop on Request, "D.O.R."

In the Greek Special Forces, the phrase for drop-outs was *eggatalipo*, which literally means, "I abandon." There is a significant difference between "I quit" and "I abandon." "To abandon" has a heavy (and always negative) connotation; therefore, soldiers are less prone to take the easy out.

Quitting may be a positive or negative change, depending on what we're quitting. For instance, quitting smoking is a positive lifestyle change. However, the word "quit" is also readily used when people walk away from important positions, commitments, or opportunities.

Language makes a difference; and the language we use now, especially since the "bail-outs", makes quitting more acceptable.

The pitfalls of quitting are many, and we must take them seriously; however, this chapter directs its focus on the rewards of perseverance.

According to Merriam-Webster dictionary, the word *Persevere* has been around since the Fourteenth Century. It means:

To persist in a state, enterprise, or undertaking in spite of counterinfluences, opposition, or discouragement

Kingdom warriors are constantly facing *counterinfluences* and *opposition*. The traps of discouragement and disappointment surround every godly pursuit and Kingdom-advancing initiative. Those who persevere and remain steadfast through all the challenges receive great revelation of the greatest force in the Universe, God's love.

The first part of Romans 5 offers some gems in regards to perseverance:

> *And not only that, we also glory in tribulations knowing that tribulation produces perseverance, and perseverance, character, and character, hope. Now hope does not disappoint, because the love of God has been poured out in our hearts by*

the Holy Spirit, who was given to us.
Romans 5:3-5

Think of the progression that unfolds after the words, "We also glory in..." First, we have tribulation—the pressures of life, the cares of this world, all the issues that weigh on us.

Tribulation produces perseverance; then perseverance produces character, which in turn produces hope. Perseverance, as a product of tribulation and a producer of character, is an integral component in this sequence.

Quitting in the face of tribulation cuts the sequence short. Persevering *through* tribulation keeps the chain intact. The last "link" of the chain is the most significant—hope.

"Now, hope does not disappoint;" instead, it points us to the "love of God [that] has been poured out in our hearts by the Holy Spirit."

How does hope, the end product of a process that begun with tribulation, point us to love?

Think of hope as one of three siblings, faith and love being the other two. These three powerful forces will endure eternally.

Now these three remain: Faith, hope, and
love, but the greatest of these is love.
1 Corinthians 13:13

The greatest of the three "sisters," love—the very personification of God—is *activated* by the presence of hope. When we choose to persevere, we make room for hope to enter; then hope makes us more keenly aware of God's love for us. What starts out as tribulation, results in a greater capacity for love within us, *if* we persevere.

I witnessed this phenomenon at work while ministering to couples in troubled marriages. Every time a husband and wife determined to persevere and try to work things out instead of choosing divorce, almost immediately their relationship would manifest a greater degree of character. They spoke more respectfully of one another and built on their strengths.

Within a few visits, the couple would express hope that their relationship would endure. Then love would show up! As couples received a revelation of God's love—the final product of the process—they began to see the treasure in one another. They found it hard to be disrespectful, selfish, or unforgiving. Reconciliation followed. I have been blessed to participate in four such restoration processes for couples that were on the verge of divorce. Perseverance was a key!

Every time we give up, we cut the process short—we don't build character, we don't attain hope, and consequently, we don't grow in our understanding of divine love.

One day, while I was in the midst of some trying circumstances, I cried out to God:

"I am so tired of fighting. When will it end?"

His response in my heart was:

"The moment you quit, you will have relief. If that's what you want, you can have it."

It was not so much what God had said that challenged me; it was what He did not say. If I *did* quit, I would enjoy temporary relief, but live with regrets afterwards.

The concept was illustrated for me within a few days, when I went for a run with my wife. It was a rough running day for me. My legs were sore and heavy; I couldn't settle into a breathing rhythm; and Danielle was going a tad faster than I was used to. I struggled the whole way. I felt worse with every step I took. Throughout the workout, I was tempted to stop running and just walk home.

The regrets associated with giving up are more tormenting and longer-lasting than "this light affliction which lasts for a moment" (2 Corinthians 4:17). On the other hand, the rewards of persevering far outweigh the sacrifices we make.

However, I knew that if I did stop running, the relief would only last for a few minutes at best. What would follow the temporary relief would be a more sustained feeling of disappointment. In other words, quitting would be far more painful than the discomfort of running.

I realized the same principle applied to every area of life. The regrets associated with giving up are more tormenting and longer-lasting than "this light affliction which lasts for a moment" (2 Corinthians 4:17). On the other hand, the rewards of persevering far outweigh the sacrifices we make.

King David was a revivalist, a reformer. Under David's leadership, Israel would be transformed for the better in numerous ways. Reformers naturally attract warriors, revolutionaries, fellow reformers; and together they plan, labor, and fight to bring transformation.

Transformation is demanding. It requires keen vision, strong leadership, and it is contingent upon the perseverance of those who are called to be agents of transformation.

David's army was comprised of mighty men. Six men in particular stood out from the rest. Their abilities and accomplishments set them apart as the "cream of the crop."

The account in 2 Samuel divides the six men into two groups. Let's look at the "lesser" of the two first:

> *Now Abishai the brother of Joab, the son of Zeruiah, was chief of another three. He lifted his spear against three hundred men, killed them, and won a name*

among these three. Was he not the most honored of three? Therefore he became their captain. However, he did not attain to the first three.
2 Samuel 23:18-19

Take note of the last sentence—"However, he did not attain to the first three."

The second man in this group—and they do seem to be presented in order of their notoriety—was Benaiah. He, too, was a "valiant man" who had "done many deeds." He killed two "lion-like heroes" from Moab, an actual lion "in the midst of a pit on a snowy day" and a "spectacular" Egyptian warrior, whom Benaiah killed with the Egyptian's own spear after wresting it out of his hand (2 Samuel 23:18-29).

These things Benaiah the son of Jehoiada did, and won a name among three mighty men. 23 He was more honored than the thirty, but he did not attain to the first three.
2 Samuel 23:22-23

There it is again: "...but he did not attain unto the first three."

Abishai, Benaiah, and a third man (of whom we know very little) performed valiantly enough to be considered among David's mighty men, and yet they fell short of making the A Team.

Hence my question:

What was it about the *first* three that set them apart, even from men like Abishai and Benaiah?

The first of the *other* three was Adino the Eznite. He seems to have earned his spot in the Elite Trio "because he had killed eight hundred men at one time" (2 Samuel 23:8).

Eleazar was the second warrior. He stood his ground and fought against the Philistines after all the Israelites had retreated. Eleazar fought long and hard, so hard that "his hand stuck to the sword" (2 Samuel 23:10). After the battle was over, Eleazar's comrades, who had initially fled, returned "only to plunder."

Last but not least was Shammah, who single-handedly defended a lentil field against the Philistines — again, *after* "the people had fled..." (2 Samuel 23:11).

> But he stationed himself in the middle of the field, defended it, and killed the Philistines. So the LORD brought about a great victory.
> 2 Samuel 23:12-13

If we look at the two groups objectively, Adino, Eleazar, and Shammah's accomplishments were not much more spectacular than those of Abishai, Benaiah, and the third man. Personally, any man that is willing to jump in the lion's den and kill it, "on a snowy day" nonetheless, gets top scores in *my* book!

What made the difference was the element of perseverance modeled by Eleazar and Shammah. They chose to stay and fight when everyone else had deserted!

God is building an army for an international end-time revival, which has the potential to far surpass all others. I assure you the warriors who will serve on the front-most of the front lines are the men and women who not only know how to fight, but who have learned to persevere.

At our church, we have a core of teenagers and young adults who are brimming with promise, potential, and destiny. They are powerfully anointed of the Lord. They have a passion for God, a heart for worship, a willingness to serve, and an ever-increasing hunger to experience and operate out of God's Glory.

Danielle and I, our staff, and our entire church family are always working to encourage, empower, and equip these emerging revivalists.

I often wonder where each of them will be in ten years. I dream about how the Lord will use them and the revolutions He will spawn through them. Though I do not know what each person will accomplish, I am certain that the extent of their influence and the longevity of their ministry will be determined, in large part, by their ability to persevere.

It is evident from several incidents in the life of David (the ones discussed above and the victory against the raiders of Ziklag—1 Samuel 30), as well as one of the parables Jesus told (of the Vineyard laborers in Matthew 20), that God is willing to extend the same compensation or reward for everyone who is on His side, even if they deserted at some point.

I have no desire to leave the battlefield and come back for the loot after others fight for the victory; nor do I have any interest in joining the vineyard workforce at the end of the day and (still) receive the same pay.

I prefer a sword in my hand, my fellow soldiers by my side, and a divinely-inspired strategy against the enemy. I intend to work and fight from start to finish; and when tribulation comes, by God's grace I intend to persevere.

I plan to have a sword stuck to my hand when the battle is over. Will you be there with me?

CHAPTER 8

HEAVEN'S TRANSFORMER

~ True humility is intelligent self-respect which keeps us from thinking too highly or too meanly of ourselves. It makes us modest by reminding us how far we have come short of what we can be. ~
Ralph W. Sockman

~ Humility makes great men twice honorable. ~
Benjamin Franklin

One of the first and most recurring lessons during Special Forces Selection had to do with pride. There is no room for individualism, arrogance, or pride in the Green Berets. From Day One, we heard the following on a daily basis:

"Pride costs lives; it will kill you or those around you."

"Heads that are lifted up will be heads that get taken out."

"You can capture the high ground by laying low to the ground all the way up."

Green Beret instructors have an uncanny ability to discern pride among recruits, and they have the responsibility and authority to take action against prideful candidates.

Walking prideful is a sure way to wipe out of Special Forces Selection; on the flip side, humility paves the way for accomplishment, recognition, and advancement.

The Bible puts it this way:

> *God resists the proud; but gives grace to the humble.*
> James 4:6

> *Therefore, whoever humbles himself as this little child is the greatest in the kingdom of heaven.*
> Matthew 18:4

The workings of God's Kingdom within every believer can be radically transformational. Through the gifts of the Holy Spirit, the anointing of God, and the revelation He releases, followers of Jesus can literally change the course of history. I liken the dynamic of God's Kingdom within us to the electricity that travels through power lines.

Power lines in the United States carry upwards of 750,000 volts of electricity. Such power would be absolutely destructive if it were to go through our homes. TVs, toaster ovens, microwaves, and every other electric appliance would explode.

The potentially-overpowering voltage in power lines is "tamed" by transformers, which convert and extract out of 750,000 volts of raw power, the energy necessary for domestic and industrial use.

I present humility as a "transformer" for the power, glory, favor, and gifting of the Lord. Humility is the virtue that enables us to release God's deposits within us in a way that can safely and effectively serve our generation. God's current of spiritual blessing within us will have maximum impact when it flows through hearts of humility.

Though we ascend to high levels of God's glory during our times of communion with Him, and though we possess high levels of authority and power in Christ, we must learn to keep our minds and hearts humble.

Paul said:

> *Let nothing be done through selfish ambition or conceit, but in lowliness of mind let each esteem others better than himself.*
> Philippians 2:3

This does not mean we should not esteem ourselves, or that we should walk in false humility, self-degradation, or unworthiness. We recognize what our Father has deposited in us, and we are aware of what He has made available to us through Jesus; yet we choose to esteem others

> When we esteem someone higher than ourselves, God makes a way for what is inside of us to impact the life of that individual.

above ourselves because that is the vehicle through which God releases what is in us, to add value to those around us.

When we esteem someone higher than ourselves, God makes a way for what is inside of us to impact the life of that individual. What we carry gets added to what he or she is carrying, and so our combined impact is multiplied.

The Apostle Paul directs our attention to the One whose life perfectly illustrates the transformer of humility:

> *Let this mind be in you which was also in Christ Jesus, who being in the form of God did not consider it robbery to be equal with God, but made Himself of no reputation, taking the form of a bond servant and coming in the likeness of men.*
> Philippians 2:5-7

Jesus consciously and purposefully made Himself of no reputation. He was a "self-made nobody." Our Lord took the form of a bond servant and came in the likeness of men. He served mankind in the most remarkable way, giving His very life for our sake:

And being found in the appearance as a man, He humbled himself and became obedient to the point of death, even the death of the cross.
Philippians 2:8

Though God may do great things for us and through us, and though He may elevate us to realms of influence and notoriety, we must choose to humble ourselves by dying daily. Jesus modeled this principle for us.

One day, He rode into Jerusalem on a donkey, and the crowds shouted, "Hosannah!" A few days later, the crowd cried, "Crucify Him!" And so Jesus went to the cross.

He was humiliated. They plucked the hairs of His beard, spat on Him, beat Him, placed a crown of thorns on His head, and nailed Him to that tree, where He died. He did that to save us and to model the ultimate act of humility: dying for someone else. He esteemed us more than Himself so all that was in Him could be released to us.

The Father's response to Christ's sacrifice reveals the reward of humility — promotion:

Therefore, God has highly exalted him, and given him the name which is above every name, that at the name of Jesus, every knee should bow, of those in Heaven and those on earth and of those under the earth and that every tongue

should confess that Jesus Christ is Lord,
to the Glory of God the Father.
Philippians 2:9

When we follow this pattern and walk in humility, and when what we carry is appropriately released, the Father lifts us up:

Let us humble ourselves before the hand
of Almighty God, that He may exalt us
in due time.
1 Peter 5:6

In the Book of Numbers, we find Moses having brought the Israelites out of Egypt and having crossed the Red Sea. They were in the desert, heading toward the Promised Land, when Miriam and Aaron began to take issue with Moses. They criticized him for marrying an Ethiopian woman.

Once they partnered with that critical spirit, Miriam and Aaron moved deeper and deeper into enemy territory. Before long, they were questioning Moses' authority and ability to lead:

Has the Lord indeed spoken only through
Moses? Has he not spoken through us
also?
Numbers 12:2

In other words, "If he would take *her* for a wife, he's not fit to lead. We should be leading instead."

I love the next part:

> *Verse 3: And the Lord heard it. Now, the man Moses was very humble. More than all men who were on the face of the Earth.*

This was Moses, the man who would raise his staff and the waters would part and the people would walk on dry ground. He would raise his staff and the water would turn to blood; the plagues would come and leave.

> Humility is the quality that enables us to release God's deposits within us in a way that can safely and effectively serve our generation.

He was carrying tremendous power, yet he was the most humble man on the Earth. The greater the authority God bestows on us, the more we must yearn to walk in humility.

> *Then He said, 'Hear now my words: If there is a prophet among you, I, the Lord, make myself known to him in a vision, I speak to him in a dream. Not so with my servant Moses. He is faithful in all my house, I speak with him face to face, even plainly and not in dark sayings, and he sees the form of the Lord. Why, then, were you not afraid to speak against my servant Moses?'"*

The most humble servant received the best compliment from the Most High God. Moses practiced and modeled humility, and he did not defend himself against Miriam and Aaron. Consequently, God intervened on Moses' behalf, and in doing so, He made a phenomenal declaration:

"I normally deal with prophets through dreams. I deal with him (Moses) face to face. Now, what was your issue with him again?!"

Jesus humbled Himself unto death and God gave Him the greatest honor ever:

> *God exalted him and gave him the name that is above every other name, that at the name of Jesus, every knee would bow and every tongue would confess, of those who were on heaven, and on and under the earth.*

Humility also plays a significant part in our assignment to draw and develop disciples for Christ. As we walk humbly before those who observe, recognize, or commend our character and accomplishments, we communicate that our success is attainable and feasible. In essence, we are saying:

"I am not better than you; I am just a vessel through which God's grace flows. He wants to channel His grace through your life as well. Follow me as I follow Christ, and see how God will use you."

> There are no stars or superheroes in the army of God. The only one who qualifies to be considered as such is Jesus, but He chose to be a servant instead.

There are no stars or superheroes in the army of God. The only one who qualifies to be considered as such is Jesus, but He chose to be a servant instead. By walking this earth in "the form of a bond servant," Jesus demonstrated how the power of God flows through yielded followers who are willing and obedient.

By seeing Christ perform signs, wonders, and miracles while in a human body like ours, we are encouraged to follow Him, emulate Him, and trust Him to work through us.

> *I tell you the truth, anyone who has faith in me will do what I have been doing. He will do even greater things than these, because I am going to the Father.*
> John 14:12

CHAPTER 9

WARRIORS IN ARMS

~ Two are better than one, because they have a good reward for their labor. For if they fall, one will lift up his companion. But woe to him who is alone when he falls, For he has no one to help him up.

Ecclesiastes 4:9-10

I was sworn in as a Green Beret on a Friday afternoon. After a forty-eight hour leave of absence, which was granted to us as a reward for completing the Special Forces selection process, I reported on Monday morning at a combat unit located at the foot of a very imposing mountain.

The moment my companions and I entered the barracks that Monday morning, we knew we were about to have a rough day. Instructors, officers, and seasoned commandos pounced on us. Within minutes after our initial entry, we were ordered to perform pushups, pull ups, and a score of other calisthenics. The drill lasted until every one of us was unable to perform any more.

Just when we thought we would finally be shown some respect for having "graduated" to warrior status, we found ourselves sweating profusely, out of breath, and belly down in the middle of a basketball court.

Several officers had gathered to witness our initiation. They repeatedly yelled in our faces, telling us we had no business being there, we should return to boot camp, we did not deserve our berets, and other such insults.

After about an hour more of exercises and intimidation, instructors and officers dismissed us to our quarters so we could sort our personal belongings. Our troubles were far from over.

About eighty seasoned Green Berets had been waiting for us. They were determined to make life as miserable as possible for us in order to weed out anyone they deemed a potential liability to the Force.

What took place over the course of that Monday constitutes the worst day of my life. By evening time, I was ready to quit, so were about a dozen other guys from my company. After all we had endured to get through boot camp, the thought of continual physical and emotional pressures at the new place brought us to a breaking point.

A few of us gathered together at night while our "tormentors" were resting. We sat down next to each other, and for a few minutes, no one said a word. We were humiliated, exhausted, and scared.

Then some of us started mumbling:

"I can't do it anymore."

"I'm getting out tomorrow."

"I don't think I can take another day of this."

Then came a moment I will never forget:

Someone muttered, "We can *do* this...if we stick together."

Suddenly, hope made an entrance into our hearts. Others piped in with similar remarks:

Sharing life with friends who have the same passion for the Cause and the same perspective of the battle is not only refreshing and edifying; it is absolutely essential.

"I'll stay if you guys stay."

"I'm glad to know I'm not alone in this."

"Others made it before us; we can do it, too."

"Let's meet here every night."

We assembled together at the same spot over the next few days. During our sessions, we licked our wounds, vented, encouraged each other, and found the resolve to continue. Consequently, none of us quit, and the friendships that were forged out of our meetings remain strong to this day.

Friendship is significant in all cultures. Everyone needs friends, especially warriors during training and front-line combat. Sharing life with friends who have the same passion for the Cause and the same perspective of the battle is not only refreshing and edifying; it is absolutely essential.

In other words, we cannot endure, contend, and maximize our potential alone—we need friends!

I offer this last chapter as a tribute to friendship, and especially my front-line comrades in God's Kingdom.

Both *Warrior Material* and my first book, *Running to the Impossible,* were birthed out of the fire. The challenges I faced while assembling the material for these books offered numerous opportunities to become discouraged, lose focus, accept limitation, and keep a cork on the passion and revelation that was burning inside me.

My friends' encouragement has made all the difference, not only in helping me persevere, but also in my choosing to write.

At the worst part of the storm, when a flood of reproach, persecution, and evil schemes threatened "life as we knew it," one friend met with me and said, "Whatever you need, whatever it takes; it's yours. Don't hesitate to ask." A pastor friend called and said, "My church and I are totally behind you!" One morning, another precious brother called:

"Marios, I'm heading to the gym to lift weights. I'm throwing a couple hundred pounds on the bench press. I'll be pumping out extra reps, just for you."

That means the world to me! Danielle and I always reserve a very special place in our hearts for the friends who stand by us, stand for us, and share life with us through the ebbs and flows of life.

> There is one major difference between military warriors and Kingdom warriors: competition.

There is one major difference between military warriors and Kingdom warriors: competition. Military training is highly competitive, especially in the Special Forces. Soldiers develop friendships within a training system, which simultaneously emphasizes two dynamics: Relentlessly outdoing one another on individual events (running, climbing, obstacle course, push-ups, etc.), and selflessly cooperating in teams during missions.

Kingdom warriors' friendships, however, are established and strengthened as believers sincerely encourage and wholeheartedly serve their friends without pretense, hidden agendas, flattery, or competitiveness. In such friendships, we are not merely *tolerant* of our friends' successes beyond or before ours; we are *exuberant!* We truly rejoice for our friends, recognizing their victories are our victories as well.

I dedicated this book to one such friend, Marie Cowell. I met Marie about a month after I had been installed as the pastor of Valley Shore. She was in her late fifties at the time; a tall, imposing, and classy lady who carried herself with great confidence and dignity. Marie loved God and people passionately, and she was very supportive of every aspect of our ministry.

When the Holy Spirit began to move in our services, Marie asked to meet with me. Up until that point, I knew very little about her personal life. We met in my office on a Monday morning. Without any small talk or preliminaries, Marie dove right into the subject she wanted to discuss:

"Marios, if you truly desire to pursue the things of God and are willing to pay the price for revival, you will need help. I believe the Lord has assigned me to help you. I would like to let you know a bit of my history."

Over the next hour or so, Marie shared the parts of her life's story which pertained to her passion for the move of God. I was deeply moved when I learned that Marie and a small group of faithful intercessors had consistently prayed for revival for more than a decade.

Marie offered to begin helping us by starting a prophetic intercession group at the church. Though Danielle and I had no idea what prophetic intercession was at the time, we agreed. Next came Marie's offer to teach a ten-week course on healing and deliverance. Then Marie began to introduce us to ministries who carried the "DNA" that was inside of us regarding the things of God.

Within six months, a radical transformation was under way at our church, and Marie was a significant catalyst. First, Danielle and I, our leaders, and close confidants learned about the importance of prophetic intercession. We met regularly with Marie's Friday night prayer group.

About a dozen of us went through the first run of the healing course with Marie. We witnessed amazing healing miracles both during the training sessions and in our Sunday services. Moreover, the relationships we began to form with other ministries bore fruit in the Body.

God was moving; we were learning; a network was beginning to form; and Marie was thrilled. Finally, after all those years of praying, she was seeing results!

Only a few months later, Marie began to suffer seizures. Within days, she was diagnosed with brain cancer. After seven months of horrible pain and suffering, Marie breathed her last and went Home.

At the beginning of her illness, I visited with Marie at the hospital and nursing homes every day for several weeks, then at least twice a week until the end. Many of our church folks helped care for Marie during the few months she was laid up at her house. Several of us took turns driving her to doctors' appointments and radiation treatments.

Whenever Marie was lucid enough to speak, she would ask questions about what the Lord was doing in our lives and at the church. She would listen intently and then offer her comments, suggestions, or advice. Then we would pray for one another. We always treasured Marie's input and our times with her, even under such trying circumstances.

One day, towards the end of our journey together, when Marie was certain only a miracle could save her, she locked eyes with me and said:

"Marios, I am going to die. I can't believe I will miss out on everything I have lived for and prayed into over the last fifteen years. This really stinks!"

As one of Marie's diligent students, I responded to her comment by boldly binding and breaking her words in Jesus' Name. Then I loosed and declared life over Marie and assured her the Lord would miraculously restore her health:

"Marie, you'll be back in church and on your front seat to the move of the Spirit in no time. Please don't say such things. Let's pray right now…"

After I prayed everything I had learned to pray over the past seven months, I opened my eyes and looked at Marie. Her look and demeanor communicated love and compassion, but also weariness and pain. As though she had not even heard my response or prayer, Marie picked up from her previous sentence:

"But Marios, you go for it, and don't hold back. God is with you. I am so happy for you. You will encounter the Lord in phenomenal ways. You and those who choose to follow you in the renewal will reap a great harvest of souls for Jesus; and I am so excited to know that!"

That was one of the last conversations I had with Marie. Within a couple of weeks, her assignment on this earth came to a close. Marie is in heaven now.

As disappointed as our dear sister felt over missing out on the fruit of what she had prayed into and helped establish, Marie was genuinely happy to know we would continue where she had left off, and go farther, deeper, and higher with Jesus. In that regard, Marie was a true Kingdom friend and a mighty warrior for Christ. I honor her as such by dedicating this book to her memory.

I believe when God determined our individual life-assignments, He also assigned us to friends, whom He raised up to help, encourage, and support us along the way. Friends have a significant role in the fulfillment of our destinies; therefore, we must carefully establish, continually cultivate, and tenaciously guard our friendships.

Whenever I leave the confines of daily battles to envision the heavenly celebration for God's final victory against the kingdom of darkness, I always picture a magnificent reunion of warriors. I see men, women, and children from every tribe, nation, and tongue. Regardless of the corner of the world we lived in and the season of history during which we served in His army, our faith in Christ united us.

Together, we trained, prayed, fought, believed, sacrificed, suffered, rejoiced, and persevered. Together, we worship our King, Jesus, the One who overcame death, hell, and the grave and defeated satan forever!

I am often encouraged by this magnificent picture of all God's warriors celebrating together. I fully believe you will be there with us on that glorious day my friend; I believe it with all my heart!

EPILOGUE

~ Homecoming means coming home to what is in
your heart.
~Author Unknown

One summer day, while our family was vacationing on the island of Cyprus, I decided to return to the Green Beret unit where I had served eighteen years earlier. Beyond my desire to check out the "old stomping grounds," I hoped to connect with someone there who might grant me permission to enter the premises, have a look around, and purchase some T-shirt and key chains from the barracks store. I took Danielle with me and drove towards Stavrovouni Mountain, the home of the Green Berets.

After almost two decades since my last day in uniform, I knew my request to enter the Unit would be a long shot. My very presence on the mountain, wearing civilian clothes, and with a beautiful young lady alongside me would be a huge challenge.

During our training, we were continually warned to look out for agents who might be spying out the Unit and another military installation nearby. I vividly remember one incident when a young couple showed up, claiming they were taking wildlife pictures. The authorities were immediately alerted and the couple was apprehended. They were indeed found to be spies!

My prospects looked grim; however, after a week or so having been laying out in the sun on Cyprus' beautiful beaches, the warrior in me was hungry for some action. I was willing to take the chance.

Around dusk that evening, after about an hour drive, Danielle and I approached our destination. A huge spotlight flashed twice, warning us to stop. I pulled up and parked about thirty yards from the gate. Danielle stayed in the car. I got out and walked towards the guard.

He was everything I had expected: tall, muscular, with an intense look, and fully armed. I greeted him and began to state the purpose for my visit. We spoke for less than a minute. What happened next was absolutely stunning!

The guard made a quick phone call. Then he informed me that the officer on duty "would be honored" to have me come in. My wife was also welcome. I ran back to the car and informed her of the situation. We decided she should remain in the car. The guard got someone to replace him, and escorted me inside.

First, we went to the barracks store, where I made my purchases; then I was ushered into the presence of the senior officer on duty. We connected right away and spoke heart-to-heart for about ten minutes.

Unbeknownst to me, the officer had called for an assembly right before I had walked in his office. By the time we finished our conversation, a large number of Green Berets were in formation, standing at ease in front of the building.

The moment we walked outside, the officer gave the command: "Ten-Hut!" As one man, all commandos lifted their right leg until it was right angles at the knee, then dropped it forcefully, Green Beret style. A loud thump and the small cloud of dust that formed brought a flood of memories and emotions. Every part of my warrior spirit was fully activated.

The officer turned to me and said:

"We honor you, Marios Ellinas. Thank you for coming to see us tonight."

Then he gave an order that all my money be returned to me.

"Your purchases are a gift from your Unit."

The soldiers stood in attention while I walked past them. The funds were returned to me, and I was escorted back to the gate.

When I got in the car, I was so overwhelmed with emotion; I didn't know where to start.

"Danielle, it was amazing...I got all this stuff...they showed me around...I met the officer...they stood in attention...I got my money back...it was amazing!"

Danielle was happy for me. She listened closely to my story and looked at everything I had bought. Then she asked a question:

"How in the world were you able to get in there without even showing any ID?"

Good question! I never thought about that detail. Moments after I had first approached the guard, things had progressed so quickly in my favor that I did process the fact I had entered one of the nation's most renowned Special Forces units without producing any identification.

Then it hit me!

"Well, Danielle, it has to do with the exchange the guard and I had upon our arrival. The things I asked and the responses I gave to his questions constitute 'insider information' that only someone who truly served in this particular Unit would have."

Even though he talked with me for less than a minute, the guard obtained enough evidence to know, beyond any doubt, I was indeed a former Green Beret who had served in that particular Unit.

Consequently, even after eighteen years since my last day in the barracks, and when I most certainly did not look like *warrior material*, the man who kept watch and the senior officer inside welcomed and honored me as a member of the Green Beret brotherhood.

Christ-followers have access into the "brotherhood" of God's Kingdom. As we surrender our lives to God by putting our faith in Jesus as Savior and Lord, and as we continue to obey Him and walk in His ways, we are recognized and esteemed in heaven. Our relationship with Jesus grants us warrior status and ensures a spectacular reception in our Lord's Glorious and Eternal Kingdom.

I was deeply touched that summer evening in Cyprus. The Green Berets treated me as one of their own. As precious as that moment was, I recognize that even the most honorable reception we can possibly fathom pales in comparison with what awaits Kingdom warriors upon their return Home:

But as it is written:
"Eye has not seen, nor ear heard,
Nor have entered into the heart of
man the things which God has prepared
for those who love Him.
1 Corinthians 2:9

Warrior Material has been a project closely connected with my heart because its content is a product of God's grace upon my life. While writing, there have been many instances when I felt a strong connection to you, the reader—moments when I knew lasting breakthrough was coming to you as a result of the love and power of God being released through the writing. Though I have no way of knowing exactly who is reading at this moment, I feel tethered to you in my heart and spirit.

I believe, as you have explored with me the various attributes that constitute a Kingdom warrior, you have journeyed right beside me in a quest to know the Living God personally and intimately.

As our time together through this book draws to a close, I ask you to consider committing or recommitting your life to Christ. If you have never asked Jesus into your heart, or if you have fallen into sin and feel distant from Him, I invite you to pray the following prayer with me:

Father in heaven,

Thank You for making a way for me to know You and have fellowship with You. I praise You for Your goodness and love. I thank You for the grace that is being poured out over me right now.

I ask Jesus Christ to come into my life. Please forgive me of my sins and release me from the bondage of my past choices and lifestyle. I commit my heart to You. I surrender my life to You. I embrace Your cross and ask for Your blood to cover me.

I am Yours; and You are mine, forever!

In Jesus' Name,

Amen!

If you are a new believer, welcome to the Family of God! If you have just recommitted your life to Him, welcome back into the fold!

I love you with the love of our Savior!

May the Father, Son, and Holy Spirit fill your life with love, joy, peace, strength, wisdom, favor, and prosperity!

I look forward to many opportunities to fight alongside you on the front-most part of the front lines!

For More Information Contact:

Marios Ellinas
Valley Shore Assembly of God
36 Great Hammock Road
Old Saybrook, CT 06475

Email: maellinas@yahoo.com

To order more copies of this book visit:

- www.warriormaterial.com

Made in the USA
Charleston, SC
01 February 2010